Advance Praise for *A Daily Spiritual Rx for Ordinary Time*

"The first Pentecost, what would it have sounded like if you were there? It would have sounded a lot like Joanna Seibert's writing. Different voices, different visions, each unique, but all coming together to create one coherent, enormously helpful spiritual tool. Weaving ideas into daily strands of thought: she is as much an artist as an author."

—Bishop Steven Charleston

"Drawing from a variety of authors, the Scriptures and her own spiritual reflections, Joanna Seibert offers us daily bits of insight to ground our lives in wisdom and to help us to live well. This book is food for the soul."

—Br. David Vryhof, *SSJE*

Joanna Seibert has given us a gift in this volume about "ordinary time"—the 29 weeks between Pentecost and Advent. Drawing from diverse Christian traditions and featuring writings by numerous authors and theologians, she shares ways to connect to the holy—in Christ, ourselves, and others—as fellow pilgrims on this journey, including contemplation, imagination, writing, listening, forgiveness, prayer, and being in nature.

—Susan Cushman, author *of Tangles and Plaques: A Mother and Daughter Face Alzheimer's, Friends of the Library*, and *Cherry Bomb*, and editor of *A Second Blooming: Becoming the Women We Are Meant to Be*, and *Southern Writers on Writing*

In her book, *A Daily Spiritual Rx for Ordinary Time,* Joanna Seibert brings together two formative spiritual practices, the church's liturgical calendar and devotional reading. This combination offers readers a rich resource for prayer and reflection, but more than that, it will cause the reader to pause and meditate in a way that makes for life and healing.

—The Reverend Dr. Frederick W. Schmidt, Rueben P. Job Chair in Spiritual Formation, Garrett-Evangelical Theological Seminary

"Dr. Seibert's book struck me as profound, abundant in wisdom and possessing enduring qualities. The real-life stories are highly instructive and captivating. The author demonstrates her authority in her field of expertise. I'll be consulting this book for guidance and advice for many years to come."

— Dr. George El-Khoury, Professor Emeritus, University of Iowa College of Medicine

Joanna deserves many accolades; she is a physician, deacon, author and spiritual advisor. However, her greatest accolade may be that she is a caring friend. A friend to her family, her parish, her larger spiritual community and to so many who cross her path. And that is what she brings to this collection of spiritual stories, passages and meditations. In her quiet and humble manner, Joanna extends her hand to each reader in friendship, daily sharing a reflection from her personal experience or a passage or meditation that has been especially meaningful. A *Daily Spiritual Rx* will touch on many of the reader's experiences. Cherish each one as if talking to a friend.

—Gary Kimmel, cherishing a friendship with Joanna that began more than 40 years ago.

Joanna's life is dedicated to healing. Her work as a radiologist testifies to an interest in our inner workings, body and soul. Thus, her insights are grounded with an incarnational view of life's journeys. She leads me to deep connections that both ground me and uplift me. In that turning, there is blessing lived out in mystery. My heart is ever grateful for her work.

—Bridget Houston Hyde, Spiritual Director

A faithful Christian, trusted spiritual director, eloquent preacher and writer, Joanna Seibert's reflections brim with wisdom and deep humility. This book is a journey through Ordinary Time; a journey that both challenges and nourishes.

—The Rev. Larry Burton, Madison, WI

A Daily Spiritual Rx for Ordinary Time:

Readings from Pentecost to Advent

Joanna J. Seibert

Other books by Joanna Seibert

A Daily Spiritual Rx for Advent, Christmas, and Epiphany

Earth Songs Press

A Daily Spiritual Rx for Lent and Easter

Earth Songs Press (Imprint: Temenos Publishing)

Healing Presence

The Call of the Psalms: A Spiritual Companion for Busy People

The Call of the Psalms: A Spiritual Companion for People in Recovery

Taste and See

Blessed Hope

Interpreting the World to the Church Vol. 1: Sermons for the Church Year

Interpreting the World to the Church Vol. 2: Sermons for Special Times

A Daily Spiritual Rx For Ordinary Time:

Readings from Pentecost to Advent

Joanna J. Seibert

A DAILY SPIRITUAL RX FOR ORDINARY TIME: READINGS FROM
PENTECOST TO ADVENT

Library of Congress Cataloging-in-Publication-Data has been applied for.

Cover Art:
"Icon of St. Joanna the Myrrh-Bearer"
Uncut Mountain Supply
www.uncutmountainsupply.com
used by permission

photograph of Dr. Seibert by Sean Moorman. seanmoorman.com

Proceeds from *A Daily Spiritual Rx for the Season after Pentecost* will be donated to
Hurricane Relief in the Central Gulf Coast and to Camp Mitchell Camp and
Conference Center in Arkansas.

Printed in the United States of America

To the clergy and staff of St. Mark's
Episcopal Church, Little Rock and Grace
Chapter of Daughters of the King who have
fed my soul during this very difficult year for
all of us.

An established author with over forty years of experience as a physician, minister, mother, retreat leader, and spiritual director, Joanna has collected daily messages from well-known spiritual authors and responds with a short discussion from her own experience particularly as it relates to spiritual direction. *A Daily Spiritual Rx* should trigger a connection to God for the reader from her own experience to sustain her for the day. Joanna addresses the most common subjects and questions brought up by people on their spiritual journeys or in spiritual direction as she shares books, readings, and experiences from both contemporary and classical writers that have most connected her to God on her personal journey.

Joanna is a frequent and well-known retreat leader, and the multiple readings on varying subjects in the book are an excellent way to journey with readers on a retreat. The book could be part of curriculum in spiritual direction classes and schools, men's and women's church groups, pastoral care classes and schools. It also speaks to those in 12-step recovery groups. Daily writings address the days in the liturgical season between the Day of Pentecost and Advent or what is also called Ordinary Time. The author has two other books in this three-part series for Advent, Christmas, Epiphany, and Lent and Easter.

Table of Contents

Pentecost

"When the Day of Pentecost had come, the disciples were all together in one place. And suddenly from heaven there came a sound like the rush of a violent wind."—Acts 2:1-2.

"…[Jesus] breathed on them and said to them, 'Receive the Holy Spirit.'"—John 20:22.

Barbara Brown Taylor[1] describes two versions of Pentecost: the gentle breeze in John, as Jesus breathes into the few disciples fearfully gathered on the night of his resurrection; and the violent wind of Pentecost that is described in Acts, as the Holy Spirit sweeps in, with tongues of fire hovering over at least a hundred people.

The disciples at the gentle wind Pentecost are commissioned to take the Spirit out into the world. The ministry assigned to the violent wind disciples is to fan the Spirit already present in the world. Taylor challenges us in our congregations to emulate the disciples in both Pentecost stories: those of the gentle breeze and those of the violent wind. Both groups are commissioned to find that Holy Spirit within themselves and others and take it out of their churches and into the world.

The same is true of the Spirit, the Christ, within us. We are called to connect to that Spirit within us and then go out and connect to the Christ in others. If we don't, we are like the disciples in John's scenario—locked up in a dreary room for fear of losing what we have. Only when we connect our Spirit to the Christ in others, do we know that peace, joy, and love that we are seeking. Our view of God also becomes larger as we become aware of the magnitude of God's creation and love.

[1]Barbara Brown Taylor, "God's Breath" in *Journal for Preachers, Pentecost 2003*, pp. 37-40.

Happy Pentecost.

Pentecost Continues

"When he had said this, he breathed on them and said to them, 'Receive the Holy Spirit.'"—John 20:22.

We are now into the season of Pentecost: remembering, celebrating that the Spirit was given to us on the Day of Pentecost. If you want to see what happened that day when the Spirit moved through a large room of people who did not have a clue what was happening, watch the video of Bishop Michael Curry's sermon at the wedding of Prince Harry and Meghan Markle on the morning of Pentecost Eve.

Usually the minister's words at a wedding are called a homily, a short sermon; but as one of the British commentators puts it, Curry's message is a true sermon—and it is all about love. He first reminds us that when two people fall in love, nearly the entire world shows up, as it did on that Saturday morning. That is how important love is.

Bishop Curry reminds us that love has the energy of fire; and his enthusiastic, passionate words are comparable to the Pentecost flames running through St. George's Chapel on that day. It appears as though Bishop Curry is so filled with the Spirit; he has to keep holding on to his lectern to stay in place.

His body language signals that he wants to move out and reach more directly toward the young couple and his congregation. As you watch people's faces, you can tell they do not understand what to do with him or his barnstorming message. They look mystified, amused, indignant, comical, questioning. Some look down at their program so others cannot see what they are thinking. Others glance at their neighbors to seek a clue from them about what is happening. Some almost fall out of their chairs! Some look at Curry as if they are mesmerized.

Perhaps the ones who seem to understand his message best are the royal wedding couple themselves—especially Meghan, who beams a radiant smile with an occasional twinkle through the whole sermon.

Bishop Curry's presentation and delivery are not given in the British style; but his message of love is true to his Anglican and African roots. He speaks out of his African American tradition, drawing from his ancestors in slavery and out of his training in an Episcopal style that Americans changed from the Anglican form. Curry speaks his truth, which comes from deep inside of him—as all these traditions mesh and kindle tongues of fire from the power of love that flames around the world.

Curry is a wonderful role model of what it is like to be filled with the Spirit. With Pentecost fire, we have no choice but to speak the truth. Many people will not have a clue what we are saying; but everyone who receives us will be changed in some way.

Bishop Curry also reminds us that the truth from God should always be about love: loving God, loving ourselves, and loving our neighbor. Period.

Happy Pentecost Season.

The First Step

"The heroic first step of the journey is out of, or over the edge of, your boundaries, and it often must be taken before you know that you will be supported. The hero's journey has been compared to a birth; it starts out warm and snug in a safe place; then comes a signal, growing more insistent, that it is time to leave. To stay beyond your time is to putrefy. Without the blood and searing and pain, there is no new life."—Diane Osbon in *A Joseph Campbell Companion* (N. Y.: HarperCollins, 1995).

People sometimes come for spiritual direction as they take that first step to becoming the person God created them to be. It is a fork in the road and always they are on a road less traveled. Sometimes the path is so undeveloped or uncared for that it is overgrown. In fact, a recognizable path can be seen only by someone who has traveled that way before. Therefore, we look for and need spiritual friends along the way.

Sometimes it may be necessary for someone to hold our hand just to get us started. Other times we see the way after just minimum help. Sometimes we need a companion for a greater distance until we become familiar with the path and adjusted to its twists and turns. The journey, and the first step, is a birth offering a multitude of opportunities for rebirth. We can always count on labor pains and a messy experience before we hear our new voice. Friends and family may have difficulty accepting our change, our new birth, the unique path we are now on.

Treasuring the journey instead of focusing on a goal can always keep us from wandering off the path.

Thomas Merton and Spiritual Direction

"The only trouble is that in the spiritual life there are no tricks and no shortcuts. Those who imagine that they can discover spiritual gimmicks and put them to work for themselves usually ignore God's will and his grace."—Thomas Merton in *Contemplative Prayers.*

Thomas Merton's concise book, *Spiritual Direction and Meditation,* is another excellent source for someone who wants to know what spiritual direction is all about. I often recommend it to spiritual friends before meeting about direction for the first time. It should also be a frequent reread for those giving spiritual direction. Merton reminds us that spiritual direction is not psychotherapy, and that directors should not become amateur therapists. He recommends that directors not concern themselves with unconscious drives and emotional problems. They should refer.

Merton's sections on meditations are classic, straightforward, and practical. He uses the story of the Prodigal Son to serve as a model for meditation, as the son "entered into himself" and meditated on his condition, starving in a distant land, far from his father. Merton also suggests the Incarnation, the birth of God into human form, as a focus for another meditation relating to birth events within our own spiritual life.

Merton emphasizes the importance of holy leisure, believing that meditation should not be work, remembering that it will take time. He reminds us of promising artists who have been ruined by a premature success, which drove them to overwork to renew again and again the image of themselves created in the public mind. An artist who is wise spends more time contemplating his work beforehand than he does putting paint to canvas; and a poet who respects her art burns more pages than she publishes.

In the interior life we must allow intervals of silent transitions in our prayer life. Merton reminds us of the words of St. Teresa: "God has no need of our works. God has need of our love." The aim of our prayer life is to awaken the Holy Spirit within us, so that the Spirit will speak and pray through us. Merton believes that in contemplative prayer we learn about God more by love than by knowledge. Our awakening is brought on not by our actions, but by the work of the Holy Spirit.

Merton also cautions us about what he calls informal or colloquial "comic book spirituality," which flourishes in popular religious literature: for example, when Mary becomes Mom and Joseph is Dad, and we "just tell them all about ourselves all day long." This may be a helpful path to God for some, but it was not Merton's path.

Catherine Marshall: *The Helper*

"When we try it on our own, we are seeking to usurp the Helper's place. The result of attempting in the flesh to convict another of sin is wreckage—defensiveness, anger, estrangement, loss of self-worth, defeatism, depression—whereas, when the Spirit does this corrective work, it is 'good' hurt, the kind that leaves no damage, that never plunges us into despair or hopelessness but is always healing in the end." —Catherine Marshall in *The Helper* (Chosen Books, 1978), pp. 214-215.

Over forty-five years ago, when our medical practice at Children's Hospital was just starting my husband and I were not as busy and could go downtown for lunch—and then perhaps browse Cokesbury Bookstore before returning to the hospital. One day I saw a book by Catherine Marshall, *The Helper,* on the front sales table for two dollars. I had remembered that she had written *A Man Called Peter* about her husband, a Scottish immigrant who became the chaplain of the United States Senate, but died a premature death. I particularly loved the movie, so I could not resist the bargain. I paid the two dollars, and it changed my life.

I did not understand concept of the Holy Spirit. Suddenly I was presented with a part of God that I could relate to who was always with me. I had had great difficulty relating to God the Father and Jesus. One was a kind old man with a beard in the sky and the other was some kind of television evangelist flipping through the Bible who wanted to save me.

For years, I held on to the Holy Spirit, the Comforter, the Helper who was always beside me, guiding me if I chose. This sustained me for a long time until I could have a deeper relationship with the other two parts of the Trinity. I am constantly amazed how God, the Holy Spirit, works: a Presbyterian minister's daughter I would never meet who was raised in Keyser, West Virginia, with my father, the son of the Methodist minister in the area; a slow time in our practice; a Methodist bookstore; a bargain table; a *New York Times* bestseller; a movie; and two dollars.

My favorite quote by Catherine Marshall was about answered prayer. She prayed for patience, and God gave her the slowest possible housekeeper. I wept when I heard about Catherine Marshall's death at age sixty-eight in 1983, just before Holy Week.

Morning Prayer

"But as for me, O LORD, I cry to you for help;
in the morning my prayer comes before you."—Psalm 88:14.

A spiritual discipline that many people use is beginning and sometimes ending the day reading and meditating on Holy Scripture. Many denominations follow a daily lectionary of Scripture readings so that over a certain period of time the reader has studied major parts of the whole Bible. In the Episcopal tradition, the *Book of Common Prayer* lists a two-year cycle of daily Lessons taken from the Psalms, the Hebrew Scriptures, a New Testament letter, and one of the Gospels for each morning and evening. By the end of each seven-week period, the reader has digested the entire Book of Psalms. After the two-year cycle, the reader has been exposed twice to all the books of the New Testament and once to pertinent portions of the Hebrew Scriptures.

We can also do the Scripture readings as part of a structured morning and evening prayer service read alone or with others. These Daily Offices provide a contemplative framework for regular use as well as offering a pattern for regular reading of the Bible. Some people use a book of daily meditations that also contains Scripture readings; others use publications such as the Methodist *The Upper Room,* the Episcopal *Forward Day By Day,* and Catholic resources *The Catholic Moment, The Word Among Us,* and *Being Catholic.* Some of these meditations are available online for reading or listening.

The Daily Offices of Morning and Evening Prayer are also online at many sites. One of the most popular office sites is *The*

Mission of St. Clare www.missionstclare.com. I use the Daily Office online from the Episcopal Diocese of Indianapolis: dailyoffice.wordpress.com.

Arthur: Literature for Pentecost

At the Still Point "is a journey of the imagination guided by poets and authors, both classic and contemporary, who have known the things of God but speak in metaphor."—Sarah Arthur in *At the Still Point* (Paraclete Press, 2011), p. 7.

At the Still Point, by Sarah Arthur is a literary compilation of daily and weekly readings and prayers designed for the long green liturgical season between the Day of Pentecost and Advent. Arthur has also published similar guides for Advent, Christmas, and Epiphany *(Light Upon Light);* and for Lent, Holy Week, and Easter *(Between Midnight and Dawn).*

In these twenty-nine weeks between the Day of Pentecost and the first Sunday in Advent, Arthur kindles our imagination as she exposes us to brief excerpts or short works of well-known writers— as well as offerings from authors we may not know but should! Arthur warns us that as we encounter some readings in this anthology, there should be an alert: "Warning: Powerful Spiritual Moment Ahead!" She suggests that we read these passages not as assignments for our English Literature class or for pleasure, but as liturgical pieces for worship and especially prayer.

Each week begins with an outline for the next seven days, comprising an opening prayer, Scripture passages, readings from literature, a place for personal prayer and reflection, and a closing prayer. Arthur suggests applying the ancient principles of *lectio divina* or divine reading that many of us have used with Scripture, now applied to selected weekly poetry and fiction writings. We read the passage, meditate on it, pay attention to a word or phrase that connects to us, and finally rest in God's presence with what we have experienced. It has been helpful to me to carry that word or phrase with me during the day, or perhaps the entire week. Since this process is now being used for literature and poetry rather than with Scripture, Arthur has christened it holy reading or *lectio sacra*.

I invite you to journey with me and with Sarah Arthur during this "Ordinary Season" with an extraordinary spiritual practice of daily worship and prayer.

The Trinity

"Trinitarian theology says that true power is circular or spiral, not so much hierarchical. If the Father does not dominate the Son, and the Son does not dominate the Holy Spirit, and the Spirit does not dominate the Father or the Son, then there's no domination in God. *All divine power is shared power.*" —Richard Rohr in *The Divine Dance: The Trinity and Your Transformation* (Whitaker House), pp. 95-96.

Robert Farrar Capon says that when humans try to describe God, we are like a bunch of oysters trying to describe a ballerina. But we can't help but try, especially as we strive to understand the doctrine of the Trinity, perhaps one of the greatest mysteries of the Christian faith.

A Greek Orthodox bishop, Metropolitan Kallistos Ware, at a lecture at a summer course at Oxford University, introduced us to Andrei Rublev's 15th-century icon, *The Trinity,* or *The Hospitality of Abraham.* It pictures the three angels who visited Abraham at the Oak of Mamre (Genesis 18:1-8) to announce the coming birth of his son, Isaac. We have interpreted it as a symbol to help visualize the mystery of the interrelationship in the Trinity of Father, Son, and Holy Spirit. Each of the figures is in a circular harmony with the other, humbly pointing to each of the others with mutual love. If we relate only to the Trinity in its separate parts, we miss the mark. The Persons are in community, transparent to each other, indwelling one another, in love with each other. They have no secrets from one another, no jealousy, no rivalry. They are teaching us how to live in community. Barbara Brown Taylor[1] describes their relationship as the sound of "three hands clapping."

The doctrine of the Trinity calls us to a radical reorientation in our way of seeing and living in the world. We are what we are *in a relationship with*. The God of the Trinity is not an *I*, but a *we;* not *mine*, but *ours*. Our belief in and understanding of the Trinity can definitely make a difference in how we drive our cars; how we fill out our tax returns; how we relate to others of different faiths, colors, and political views; how we stand in relation to war; how we treat the person sitting across the aisle from us, as well as those living across the Interstate and outside our country's borders. Richard Rohr's and Barbara Brown Taylor's thoughts are excellent to mediate on when we are having a conflict with another person, when the Christ within us is having difficulty seeing the Christ in another.

[1]Barbara Brown Taylor, "Three Hands Clapping" in *Home By Another Way* (Cowley), pp. 151-154.

Serenity Prayer

"God, Grant me the Serenity to accept the things I cannot change,
Courage to change the things I can,
And Wisdom to know the difference." —Reinhold Niebuhr.

My grandmother kept a copy of the Serenity Prayer on her bathroom mirror. Today I honor her by doing the same. I can remember visiting her as a young girl and reading the prayer in her bathroom every morning. What I especially remember is that I thought, "This is the most ridiculous prayer! If there is a problem, I know if I try hard enough, I will be able to solve or fix it!"

Many years later, many trials later, I have learned the hard way the truth of the Serenity Prayer. There are so many things I cannot change. In fact, the only thing I *can* change is myself and my reactions to other people and situations. I cannot change others. I try to share my firsthand experience with spiritual friends; but so often others like myself need a firsthand rather than a secondhand experience to see this truth.

I wonder if it took my adoring grandmother as long as it did me to discover and learn to live the truth.

I wonder if she had as many setbacks as I so often do—thinking I can change situations and others.

"The Examen builds on the insight that it's easier to see God in retrospect rather than in the moment." —James Martin in *The Jesuit Guide to (Almost) Everything: A Spirituality for Real Life* (HarperOne, 2010), p. 97.

"Rummaging for God" in our lives.

One of the central practices in Jesuit devotion—the one that Ignatius of Loyola considered indispensable—was the prayer of Examen. Ignatius felt that the key to spiritual growth was to cultivate an awareness of when and where God had been present for us in the day's course. It was so important, in fact, that he urged his followers to do the Examen, even if it cost them the little time that they might have for prayer.

One writer calls this "rummaging for God" in our lives. Rummaging is a wonderful, commonplace activity we have all often resorted to when we have lost something: car keys, phones, and umbrellas being among my personal favorites over the years.

The Examen is a practice that tells us something important about the spiritual life: Spiritual practice is preeminently about cultivating a sense of God's presence. It isn't about devotional piety or about the number of hours we spend in overtly religious activity. It isn't an anxious, endless effort to earn the love of God. The spiritual life is about cultivating an habitual awareness of God's presence that shapes and informs our lives.

Ignatius recommends two questions:

One: What were the events in your life today—the moments, conversations, and choices—that drew you closer to God and to others in love?

Two: What were the events in your life today—the moments, conversations, and choices—that drove you away from God and others?

The answers to those simple questions invite us to evaluate our lives from a spiritual center. They are not about what feels good and what doesn't feel good. Some things—such as addiction—feel good at first, but they invariably isolate us from God and others; and, by contrast, some things that don't feel good, like asking for forgiveness, can actually draw us closer to God and to those around us.

Instead, these questions raise our awareness of how patterns, habits, and choices shape our lives and how, armed with that knowledge, we can learn to be more readily available both to God and to others.

Rummaging around in our lives for God can be the source of inspiration, encouragement, strength, gratitude, and a renewed sense of spiritual purpose. That's not a bad result for an activity that usually leads to the discovery of dust bunnies and lost umbrellas.

—The Reverend Dr. Frederick W. Schmidt.

De Mello: Intercessory Prayer

"It is extremely important that you become aware of Jesus and get in touch with him at the beginning of your intercessory prayer. Otherwise your intercession is in danger of becoming not prayer, but an exercise of remembering people. The danger is that your attention will be focused only on the people you are praying for and not on God."—Anthony de Mello in *Sadhana: A Way to God* (Image Books), p. 126.

De Mello's book has had a major impact on my spiritual practices. The awareness exercises of my surroundings, my body, my senses have been the most practical avenues of learning how to experience God's presence. I knew of these exercises before, and tried them without success; but for some reason they now have become an important spiritual practice to me.

One more lesson to remember: Spiritual practices that were not meaningful in the past can become important later on.

De Mello suggests that rather than trying to envision the face or clothes of Jesus, we might seek a sense of Jesus in the shadows, calling him by as many names as we are led to. He recommends imagining Jesus in our prayers in an *empty chair* beside us. This can be one of the most consistent ways of experiencing the presence of Christ.

These exercises for intercessory prayer can change the way we pray and talk about prayer to others, as we remember Jesus as the great intercessor; imagine Jesus' presence directly beside us; and visualize those we are praying for with Jesus, laying hands on them.

The book's last prayers deal with turning desires and prayers over to God one at a time—praising God at all times for everything, good and bad. This also can change our prayer practice and how we live our lives.

De Mello invites us to live and pray intimately, becoming a part of the grand mystery of God's love for us and all creation in the present moment. He believes that this precious now, the present moment, is where God meets us.

Rohr: Nature

"If you scale chronological history down to the span of one year, with the Big Bang on January 1, then our species, *Homo sapiens,* doesn't appear until 11:59 p. m. on December 31. That means our written Bible and the church appeared in the last nanosecond of December 31. I can't believe that God had nothing to say until the last nanosecond."—Richard Rohr, Daily Meditation, Center for Action and Contemplation.

We are staying at a favorite hotel by the Mississippi River. We watch the sun give its last hurrah of pink and orange as it sets over the churning water, racing to New Orleans and the Gulf of Mexico. We follow a rare treat of the migration of a super full moon that is brighter and larger, appearing to be closer to the earth than usual. It finally sets over the north shore of the Mississippi River and quickly disappears into a cloud bank at early dawn.

There is a gentle breeze blowing the last of the leaves from their trees near the water's edge. The cottonwood leaves seem to be the last holdouts. As the wind blows their palm shapes, they appear to be clapping, praising their Creator—in awe of the spectacle we have seen just before their own last flight.

Nature is telling us something. There is still amazing beauty in the world. Something greater than we can ever imagine fashioned it all. All of nature seems to give thanks and honor its Creator. Dare we consider joining the dance and doing the same?

Esther Harding: Change

"We cannot change anyone else; we can change only ourselves, and then usually only when the elements that are in need of reform have become conscious through their reflection in someone else." —M. Esther Harding in *The 'I' and the 'Not-I': A Study in the Development of Consciousness* at InwardOutward.org.

Esther Harding was a British American considered to be the first significant Jungian Analyst to practice in this country. Her first book, *The Way of All Women* (1975), was one of the first books I read in my early days of seeking to connect to a feminine spirituality.

President Jimmy Carter wrote recently about getting to the place where we can give thanks for our difficulties. That is almost impossible; but I can see his reasoning a little more clearly in Esther Harding's writings. We wear our character defects and self-centeredness like an old bathrobe that is ugly and tattered, but comfortable and a known entity. Our habitual manner of life has become our familiar identity. We can only recognize these defects and behavior patterns in others, as we are repulsed by them—and finally identify them as our own. Our behavior and reaction to the world is keeping us from our connection to God.

I continually am amazed how God uses everything, *everything* to bring us back to God's love, to connect us to the God within us and within our neighbor. We find out what is blocking us from God's love by first seeing the barriers in someone else and realizing how unbeautiful they are.

At some point, when the time is right, I can share Harding's insights with spiritual friends who also are suffering. I, as well, have spiritual friends who listen to me when suffering brings awareness that opens up a crack of light into my own life.

Holy Smoke

"And the smoke of the incense, with the prayers of the saints, rose before God from the hand of the angel."—Revelation 8:4.

I slowly stand up from my seat next to the Bishop's chair near the altar at Holy Spirit Episcopal Church in Gulf Shores, Alabama, as the organist plays the prelude to the closing hymn, "Lift High the Cross." The music is uplifting, but suddenly I am transported and raised to another space. There is an unfamiliar burning smell in the air. I look up and see two almost straight lines of black smoke rapidly rising at least a foot above the altar—and just as quickly disappearing into the air in front of the congregation.

I am aware, as the acolyte in the white alb passes by me to reach for the silver processional cross, that she just extinguished the two candles on the glass altar.

This smell is different from what I usually perceive at the end of the service. For me this is an especially holy smell, accompanied by an uplifting holy smoke, stronger than incense. It is raw, attention getting, signaling that something has happened. The few in the front rows of the congregation can see the black smoke; but the smell probably persists only around the altar. By verse two of the hymn, as the crucifer leads the choir members in their blue cassocks and white surplices out of the church, I realize what this is all about.

The Altar Guild of Holy Spirit uses real candles, not the oil candles that I am familiar with in many of the churches I visit or serve. This is the smell and smoke from extinguished candle wax.

This is also the residual fragrance after a session of spiritual direction with seekers as they depart. I light a candle at the beginning of a session when I am doing spiritual direction to symbolize our meeting as holy, as we care for our souls. I extinguish the candle at the end of our time to symbolize the passing of what we have shared. I know our time together as spiritual friends is holy work, just as our Eucharist together on Sunday is a holy time.

The smell and the smoke tell me that whatever has happened is now being lifted up, spreading into the air of our surroundings, our universe. The Word we had together has now moved away from the altar or our meeting place and out into the world. We can no longer see the smoke, but it is there. I experience the smell only briefly, but it is an icon of what is happening.

The holy Word has moved on with its healing blessing out into the world, making a difference in all our wounded spaces. Bless the Altar Guild of Holy Spirit for teaching me a little more about the movement of the holy.

Interruptions

"While visiting the University of Notre Dame, I met with an older professor and while we strolled he said with a certain melancholy, 'you know, my whole life I have been complaining that my work was constantly interrupted, until I discovered that my interruptions were my work.'"—Henri Nouwen in *Reaching Out: The Three Movements of the Spiritual Life* (Image Books, 1975), p. 52.

This has been my experience. I have an agenda, but I am slowly, often painfully learning that God most often meets me in the interruptions in my life not on my agenda. There is that call from a friend or family member when I think I am too busy to talk. For me this is a sure sign that I am in trouble, losing priorities of what life is all about, if I cannot stop and talk. Interruptions are like a stop or yield sign to go off script and listen for a grace note. Nouwen calls them opportunities, especially opportunities for hospitality and novel experiences. When I come back to a project after an interruption, I usually have fresh ideas; but there is that false idea that keeps ever lurking and speaking in my ear that if I stop, I will lose my creativity or my train of thought.

Interruptions are also a reminder of how powerless we are. If we think we are in charge, the interruptions remind us that this is a myth. When I seal myself off and refuse to respond to anything but what is on my agenda, I become exponentially isolated. My world, my God, become too small. I become the center of the universe and fossilized. I develop a high hubris titer.

Name Day: June 24

"On the eighth day they came to circumcise the child, and they were going to name him Zechariah after his father. But his mother said, 'No; he is to be called John.' They said to her, 'None of your relatives has this name.' Then they began motioning to his father to find out what name he wanted to give him. He asked for a writing tablet and wrote, 'His name is John.' And all of them were amazed." —Luke 1:59-63.

If your name is John or some derivative, June 24 is your name day. We also celebrate it as the birthday of John the Baptist. In some countries such as Greece, this is even more important than your regular birthday. When our daughter, Joanna, and her dad were in Greece on this, her name day, their guide Maria did not charge them for taking them around that day. When others heard that it was her name day, they gave her gifts.

Just as important as this name day is to our family is the remembrance that June 24 is the birthday of Bob, my husband's father, who showed us and our children so much unconditional care and love. More and more in my life, I find it important to remember people who taught us about unconditional love. As we remember the person, we can feel that love they brought into our lives.

Consider finding out about your name, how you got your name, and even your name day.

On June 24, I also remember my grandparents, Joe and Anna, as I was named after them. Again, these were two people who taught me about love without conditions. I was the "apple of their eye." They loved me no matter what I did. They did not always condone what I did, but they still loved the sinner. Through their love, I learned about the unconditional love of God.

Honor and remember those who have brought the presence of love into your life. My experience is that in bringing them back into our memory, we can still feel and experience that love—even if they are not with us and are now living in eternal life. The God of my understanding does not give us this love and then stop it at death. Love lives on. Love never dies.

Sighs Too Deep for Words

"Likewise the Spirit helps us in our weakness; for we do not know how to pray as we ought, but that very Spirit intercedes with sighs too deep for words."—Romans 8:26.

Trent Palmer reminds us in a recent post about this Daily Lectionary reading from Romans[1]—how this Romans passage has changed his prayer life. He is trying to wait for the Holy Spirit to lead him in prayer, knowing that God is doing for all of us far more than we can pray for or imagine ourselves.[2] I need to hear this from The Daily Lectionary, Romans, *The Book of Common Prayer,* and Trent each week.

My prayers, especially for others, are a way to move out of the orbit I live in and know there is something going on greater than my mind, my feelings, my world. The space I live in is only a minor piece of God's world, perhaps like a grain of sand. But still, the God who loves us so much cares deeply about us, each grain of sand, each hair of our head, and loves us beyond what we can imagine. It is comforting to know that no matter what we pray for; the Spirit is there to guide our prayers. Sometimes I try to remember this by leaving a period of silence in prayer, followed by a few sighs of my own, hoping they will catch up with the sighs of the Holy Spirit!

I have friends who say to God, "I turn this day over to you for your care." I admire them. I take more than ten words to turn over my day as well as those I care for and those I pray for. That is why intercessory prayer has become so important in my life. I aim for the shorter versions, but for today I am praying in long division.

[1]Trent Palmer, "Morning Reflection" from St. Paul's Episcopal Church, Fayetteville, Arkansas, Monday, July 9, 2018.

[2]"Prayer for Those We Love," *Book of Common Prayer*, p. 831.

Cushman: Praying with Icons
Guest Writer Susan Cushman

"I have chosen icons because they are created for the sole purpose of offering access, through the gate of the visible, to the mystery of the invisible. Icons are painted to lead us into the inner room of prayer and bring us close to the heart of God."—Henri Nouwen in *Behold the Beauty of the Lord: Praying with Icons* (Ave Maria Press, 1987).

For four years in a row, in the 1980s, Henri Nouwen spent time at a spiritual retreat in France. Each year, someone placed an icon in the room where he would be staying. At the end of these visits, he wrote a book about his experiences with these icons—*Behold the Beauty of the Lord: Praying with Icons*. He gazed at these four icons for hours at a time, and, after patient, prayerful stillness on his part, they began to speak to him. As a man who loved the art of Michelangelo, Rembrandt, and Marc Chagall, he could have chosen any of these Western treasures for his meditations. But he chose icons. When I became an Orthodox Christian, I embraced icons as "windows to heaven," and have prayed before them for many years. As an iconographer, I have written many icons—some commissions, some as gifts, and some that I have kept in our home—and found the process to be very much like a prolonged prayer. These images of Christ, the Mother of God, and various saints and angels, draw my hear to God in a way that nothing else does. In addition to the "set" prayers I pray in the morning and evening, sometimes I pray specific prayers to saints depicted in the icons. Here is one to the Mother of God:

"Forasmuch as thou art a well-spring of tenderness, O Theotokos, make us worthy of compassion; Look upon a sinful people; Manifest thy power as ever, for hoping on thee we cry aloud unto thee: Hail! As once did Gabriel, Chief Captain of the Bodiless Powers." —St. John of Damascus, quoted in "Icons Will Save the World" in *First Things* (12/20/2007) by Susan Cushman.

—Susan Cushman

Image Gently

"Relationship is not a project, it is a grace."—Thomas Moore in *Soul Mates: Honoring the Mysteries of Love and Relationship* (HarperCollins, 1994), p. 256.

My friend, Marilyn Goske, who also is a pediatric radiologist, has spearheaded a campaign called *Image Gently* to decrease radiation to children in diagnostic radiology. This organization encourages physicians to use the least amount of radiation when performing tests on children. It applies to conventional X-rays, fluoroscopy, interventional radiology, nuclear medicine, computed tomography, dentistry, cardiac imaging, and imaging in the setting of minor head trauma. It is the organization's aim to make physicians, technologists, and nurses aware of the amount of radiation being used, as well as the importance of reassuring parents about any of their concerns. This educational program entails communication with all those directly involved in these studies, and all medical organizations that support them. It has had overwhelming success, with over 63,000 pledges, to take part in this program.

Marilyn is showing us how we can change the world by communicating and dialoguing with all people who share a special interest. It involves trying to solve a problem, talking together, working together, celebrating when answers come, and honoring those who are bringing the vision to reality. In this way we are seeing the power of community.

I realize how important this could be in our spiritual lives. We find more answers to our spiritual questions in community; whereas often we cannot understand our concerns by ourselves.

Yesterday I met with my spiritual director, who helped me understand a dream that had baffled me for days. Each day in the early morning, I go back to the dream and uncover another insight as though she, and all those who have taught me about dream work, are still guiding me.

We also have many parts of ourselves: inner masculine, inner feminine, the child within, and so many more. When we can see them as helpful voices rather than unwanted adversaries, especially coming from the weaker parts of ourselves, they reveal answers. It is in our weakness, in our vulnerability, especially in community, that God the Holy Spirit creeps in and helps us discern a path—where before we saw only a jungle.

In community, we image gently.

Visio Divina

"The experience of praying with icons and other images is quite different than praying with words." —Christine Valters Paintner in *Illuminating Mystery: Creativity as a Spiritual Practice, Reflections in Word and Image* (Abbey of the Arts Press, 2009).

God speaks to us in many ways—through relationships, our experiences, sacred texts such as the Bible, and other avenues. *Visio divina,* Latin for *divine seeing,* is praying with images to listen to God's words. It is similar to *lectio divina,* Latin for *divine reading,* in which we pray using sacred reading such as Holy Scripture. There are four steps we can follow to practice *visio divina:*

1. Sit quietly, close your eyes, and be aware of your breathing. Practice a body scan. Open your eyes and look at the image of art slowly, seeing colors, people, places, and things. Stay with the image for one to two minutes. Jot down a few words about the image.

2. Close your eyes and breathe. Open your eyes. Take another, deeper look. Is there movement? Are there relationships? Use your imagination. What is the story? Can you place yourself in the story and in the image? Do you see deeper meanings than what is on the surface?

3. Respond to the image with prayer. Does the image take you to an experience, or remind you of a person or issue for which you want to offer thanksgiving or intercession? Offer that prayer to God.

4. Find your quiet heart center. Stay connected to your body. Breathe deeply. Relax your shoulders, arms, and legs. Rest in this quiet. Imagine God praying in you. God prays beyond words.

—From Kathryn Shirey, "How to Pray with 'Eyes of the Heart' Using *Visio Divina*" at www.KathrynShirey.com.

Abundance

"The church is the only community in the world that has as its central symbolic act, an act that is called, 'Thanks.' The Eucharist. You know Eucharist is Greek for 'Thanks.' And participation in the Eucharist is an act of gratitude for the abundance that the creator God gives to the world.

And I think that the neighborly economy can only be funded by gratitude. It is all a gift! I did not make any of it, produce any of it, it is a gift! But the extraction economy wants to think, 'It's mine! I made it, I own it, I can do what I want, I don't have to be grateful to anybody.'

Which leads me to think that participation in the Eucharist is the most subversive thing we can do.

But notice what the long history of the church has done to the Eucharist. It has siphoned off its danger into something about sin and salvation and getting right with God, rather than a meal for the neighborhood."

—Walter Brueggemann in *InwardOutward Daily Quote, August 23, 2018, InwardOutward.org, Church of the Saviour.*

Brueggemann reminds us of something we so often forget about the Eucharist. Christ called all to the Welcome Table, and this should be the center of our worship. Weekly or daily Eucharist is an experience of abundance. There is always enough bread and wine and always some left over. The Eucharist is a reminder of an exceptional gift, the love of God for each of us and for all.

Remembering that we are giving thanks for God's great gift of love, remembering that this is a table for all, remembering this is a table of abundance, remembering that this is an assurance that we have been given a life of abundance through Christ that can make all the difference in how we receive the Eucharist and how we live our lives.

Storm Warnings

"Jesus also said to the crowds, 'When you see a cloud rising in the west, you immediately say, 'It is going to rain'; and so it happens. …You know how to interpret the appearance of earth and sky, but why do you not know how to interpret the present time? And why do you not judge for yourselves what is right?'"—Luke 12:54-57.

I sit and watch a storm come up the beach in the early morning. The sun is out and there are blue skies to the east, but to the west the sky is grayer. Clouds move overhead. Sometimes this dark overhead carpet seems so close I think I can touch it. Fishing boats come back into port to weather the coming storm. Birds take shelter. The great blue heron moves inland. The pelicans are nowhere to be seen. The mighty osprey is the last to give up looking for one more meal before she moves back to her nest. A violent wind precedes and announces the pivotal event, the driving rain, which is almost horizontal.

Jesus reminds us we see signs in our own life that indicate storms may be coming. Our children act out or their grades at school drop. We get random hints that a project is not going well; but we are too busy to take care of that matter right now. *Later. Too many other things going on.* We remember how a certain food affected us in the past, but we eat it anyway. Our clothes no longer fit, but we do not change our eating, our exercise habits, or our lifestyle. We ignore a pain that is a sign that some body part needs attention.

The same is true in our spiritual life. Our prayer life seems dry. We cannot remember our dreams. We can no longer write. All we read seems dull and uninteresting. We think of every excuse not to attend corporate worship. We stop going outdoors. It is too hot. Too cold. Too sunny. Too cloudy. We stop talking with friends. We isolate ourselves.

In medicine, a sign is an outward or objective appearance that suggests what is going on—like the red butterfly rash across the nose characteristic of *lupus erythematosus*. A symptom describes something subjectively experienced by an individual, such as the fatigue of lupus, or pain with a urinary tract infection, which requires some interpretation.

We constantly are given signs and experience symptoms in both our outer and inner life that can direct us. God never abandons us. We are called only to keep ourselves "in tune" to see and hear. Spiritual directors, spiritual friends, spiritual practices all are gifts that can help us along this journey. They assure us we are not alone, and that a directional move or change in course may be needed in our outer or inner life.

My own experience, however, is that I am so much like that osprey, waiting until the very last minute before I surrender to something greater than myself.

Our Story

"The name is strange. It startles one at first. It is so bold, so new, so fearless. It does not attract, rather the reverse. But when one reads the poem this strangeness disappears. The meaning is understood." —J .F. X. O'Connor, S. J., in *A Study of Francis Thompson's Hound of Heaven* (John Lane Company, 1912), p. 7.

Once a week I meet with a group of friends who share how God is working in their life. I go to this meeting on Saturday morning because I believe in miracles, and that belief is always affirmed by what I hear and see. These are people once caught in addiction, who thought there was no way out—but somehow, through the grace of God and with the help of community, found a new life. I give up my Saturday morning to meet with some people I have seen for years and others I have never met before. There are people from all walks of life, many I would not have known otherwise.

This Saturday, many people talk about the time when they realized there might be a way out of their old lifestyle. They call it a moment of clarity. Many were desperate. Some just knew this was not the path they would ever choose, but there they were.

When they came to the group for help, they were at first very uncomfortable. I came to this 12-step group around Thanksgiving. I can remember seeing posters about a Thanksgiving potluck. I remember thinking *I don't enjoy being here, and goodness knows I don't want to eat with these people as well!* Today, almost thirty years later, most of the people I go out to eat with are those I met through this community!

Many talked about how they did not understand what gave them the courage to come to this meeting. Story after story revealed that there is something greater than all of us—caring, loving us, and calling us to become the persons we were created to be. I also see this phenomenon in people who come for spiritual direction. Something is calling us out of our God hole—the God, the Christ within us, who, deep down inside of our being, makes us aware that we are unconditionally loved.

In 1893 Francis Thompson wrote a 182-line poem about his experience of being "hounded" by God and called it *The Hound of Heaven*. I could not have written a better description.

Darkness and Light and Candles and Prayers

"If I say, 'Surely the darkness will cover me, and the light around me turn to night,' darkness is not dark to you, O Lord; the night is as bright as the day; darkness and light to you are both alike."
—Psalm 139:11-12.

At the five o'clock contemporary service every Sunday night at St. Mark's Episcopal Church, the darkened nave is illuminated only by tea light candles on the altar in front of a large icon. After the usual Prayers of the People with a Leader and People response, they invite members of the congregation to come up and light a candle in front of the altar as they say a silent prayer of intercession. Tonight's pianist plays music from the Taizé community, as almost all the members of the congregation come forward.

While I remain in the chair behind my harp, I experience the scene as a Spirit-filled synthesis of corporate and individual intercessory prayer. I watch men and women and sometimes children walk silently up to light their taper and put it in an enormous earthenware bowl filled with sand. I know a few of the prayers that may be on some hearts. There are many people I do not know, much less what they are praying for; but I see faces displaying earnest emotion, and even sometimes silent tears. Even when I do not perceive their prayers, I can feel their power and maybe even their connection. There is a stream of people connecting to God in prayers for others, and sometimes for themselves.

The light from the many candles now brings brighter light to the nave of the church. The scene has become its own icon for teaching us what happens when we pray. Out of the darkened nave, prayers germinate and are born to transform the darkness into light. I keep remembering that C. S. Lewis once wrote that he "prayed not to change God, but to change himself." These silent prayers being transported by candlelight are changing the appearance of the church and the pray-ers, and certainly they are changing me.

Practicing and Preaching and Fear

"If mainstream Christianity has steadily lost force and credibility, I wonder how much might be attributed to that we preach one gospel and live another. We preach the Good Samaritan and lock our church doors. We preach the lilies of the field and allocate large amounts of our monthly paychecks to pension and insurance plans."—Cynthia Bourgeault in *Mystical Hope* (Cowley, 2001).

This is the old story of practicing what we preach. We talk one way, but act another. My experience is that much of what we do is unconscious. We see ourselves as good and caring people. We know a certain belief is part of our core values; but our society speaks against it or does not value it. This gives us excuses or wiggle room so we don't have to follow through.

My experience is that fear and the scarcity/zero-sum mentality most often keep us from being this person God created us to be, not being able to act on what we know at our core is true. We fear we will not have enough money. We worry that someone will break in and steal what we already have. We fear our health will fail. We experience anxiety over the thought of being left alone and abandoned.

Being grateful, expressing thanks for what we have, is one of the best ways to journey out of a fear-based life. We have been given a daily reminder of how much God cares for us and loves us. When I am most fearful, I rise early in the morning and watch the sunrise. Out of deep darkness comes overwhelming light. God gives us a new hope, a fresh start, each day. Out of our darkness comes resurrection when we have the courage to look fear in the eye and realize the blessings we have been given. Living out of gratitude rather than fear can help us practice what we preach.

Daily Protection Prayer

"May the guiding hands of God be on my shoulders,

may the presence of the Holy Spirit be on my head,

may the sign of Christ be on my forehead,

may the voice of the Holy Spirit be in my ears,

may the smell of the Holy Spirit be in my nose,

may the sight of the company of heaven be in my eyes,

may the speech of the company of heaven be in my mouth,

may the work of the church of God be in my hands,

may the serving of God and my neighbor be in my feet,

may God make my heart his home,

and may I belong to God, my Father, completely."

—Lorica of St. Fursa (Fursey), 7th Century, Translation composite, from Facebook Page of the Rev. Dr. Frederick Schmidt.

Fred Schmidt puts a prayer on his Facebook page almost every day. I cannot get this one out of my mind. St. Fursa was an Irish monk who was among the first to spread Christianity to Anglo-Saxon England in the seventh century. A "Lorica" is a protection prayer in the Irish Celtic tradition, often used before going to battle. It may have come from the original Latin word *lorica,* meaning breastplate or armor. This prayer may have been inspired by Paul's writing in Ephesians 6:11 to "put on the whole armor of Christ."

As modern Christians, we stand to learn much from the Celts. We have a treasury of their wisdom, because writing and education were so important to them. I think of others who worshiped God, but of whose traditions we know nothing, because their *experience*—and not the writing—was primary to them. We need both.

This form of prayer should meet us as we wake up in the morning, maybe with that first cup of coffee or tea, or even before.

We may need to go back to it during the day, leaving a copy in a convenient place so as not to miss putting on "the whole armor of God." Sometimes life *does* seem like going into battle. My experience is, however, that when prayers such as this one become part of our being, we recognize that the battle is over and that love has already won.

The Day after July 4th
"America! America! God mend thine every flaw,

confirm thy soul in self-control, thy liberty in law."

—Katherine Lee Bates

This coming Sunday nearest the fourth of July we will have a patriotic hymn sing along after church. One of my favorites is the music to Katherine Lee Bates poem, "America the Beautiful." "O beautiful for spacious skies for amber waves of grain." Bates wrote the hymn after she arrived in a prairie wagon on top of the 14,000-feet Pike's Peak near Colorado Springs in the summer of 1893.

I became connected to the poem and the hymn when I helped plan a pediatric radiology meeting at nearby Colorado Springs in 1994. I took a sabbatical from Children's Hospital for six months to plan the international pediatric radiology meeting. I had much help from people all over the world, but I also had a touch of what Parker Palmer calls "functional atheism," believing I was the "only" one who needed to get most of the work done.

After a year of planning and everything was ready, I vividly remember sitting in a board meeting in May at the event hotel just before the conference was about to begin. I looked out of the adjacent wide bay window, and observed, to my horror, the beginning of the last snow of winter, in May! I had planned in detail a multitude of outdoor activities that now would never see the light of day. I now keep a beautiful picture of snow on the tulips in front of the hotel to remind me of how little in life I can control.

There were a multitude of other hiccups. We recorded speakers for a meeting video. One speaker did not like his recording and required us to redo his filming at least five times. I will always be indebted to Marilyn Goske, whom I had casually asked to watch over the videoing of the speakers. She patiently stayed with the speakers and missed the whole meeting to get this done. Another hiccup was our evening entertainment after dinner. We had scheduled the Air Force Academy Cadet Choir. Then without warning they were called to maneuvers. Our meeting planner booked a local children's chorus. I worried that this would be amateurish and poorly performed. As you might expect, they were the most charming, talented and poised children performers I have ever seen. They ended their concert by going to individual members of the highly educated, sophisticated audience and held their hands and sang directly to them. We all gave them a standing ovation through our tears, remembering that the children we serve as physicians can teach us so much about life as well as "American the Beautiful."

I also learned from this meeting that no matter how hard I try, I am not in charge, that God provides amazing people around me who will take over situations that are overwhelming. I especially learned after dinner that when a door unexpectedly closes, the next door that opens often is surprisingly magnificent.

Nouwen: Healing Our Hearts Through Forgiveness

"How can we forgive those who do not want to be forgiven? But if our condition for giving forgiveness is that it will be received, we seldom will forgive! Forgiving the other is an act that removes anger, bitterness, and the desire for revenge from our hearts. Forgiving others is first and foremost healing our own hearts."—Henri Nouwen in *Bread for the Journey* (HarperSanFrancisco, 1997).

Recently I was with an amazing group of women in Searcy, Arkansas, as we talked about forgiveness. One of the first questions from two of the women was, "How can I forgive someone who has harmed me or someone I love when they do not see that they have done any wrong?"

These are the hardest hurts for me to forgive as well. We think we are doing fine; but then we hear how the people involved see no wrongdoing on their part, and an angry dragon rears his head again. This anger is nothing like our initial reaction; but it still endangers our body, our mind, and our soul. We are allowing the people and the situation to continue to harm us—unless we can transform that energy into something useful for our body and the world.

I think of a small church-related school that I, and many others, were involved with that was closed overnight. After several years, most of us have worked through the disappointment and have moved on. We will all carry a scar; but for the most part the wound is healing.

Most of us decided that if we cannot forgive those involved in the closing, or those who did nothing to prevent it, they are still hurting us. They take up space in our minds, our life, our bodies, and our relationship with others. We all have prayed to transform the enormous amount of energy generated by this hurt into something positive. We all are now discovering gold—deep down below this pain.

I often go to a place where I remember the children and teachers and school board singing and carrying small lighted candles as they walked out into the world, in pairs, at the conclusion of the school's last graduation. What I cherish every day is the light that each of those involved at this school now bring to so many other schools, homes, churches, and places of work. We have been sent out to share what we learned from that experience: the relationships, the love, the kindness to others, the acceptance of differences, the belief in a very loving God.

There was so much light radiating from that school. That is why it was so hard to leave. But now we are commissioned to carry the light we received there out into the larger world. We can make a difference in so many other lives, and so many have been doing just that.

Faith

"Faith means receiving God, it means being overwhelmed by God. Faith helps us to find trust again and again when, from a human point of view, the foundations of truth have been destroyed. Faith gives us the vision to perceive what is essential and eternal. It gives us eyes to see what cannot be seen, and hands to grasp what cannot be touched, although it is present always and everywhere."
—Eberhard Arnold in *Why We Live in Community* (Plough, 2014).

Faith is believing in something we cannot see or understand. The mind takes us to a certain level of belief; but then faith must be present for us to take the leap from there. My favorite quote about faith, attributed to a multitude of people, is: "The opposite of faith is not doubt, but certainty." If we are so certain about something, we have crossed back over that line, away from the place where faith abides.

This gives all of us doubters great comfort. In fact, we know that our doubts lead us into a deeper faith—across the line, down new pathways, sometimes even onto major highways. We may take a wrong turn, or run a red light and hit someone, or just become completely lost. Then that stranger who met us on the road to Emmaus shows up. He may remind us of a quote from Scripture that had been meaningful to us in the past. He may ask us if we remember how we have been cared for continually by the God of our understanding, as well as by God's stand-ins, our community and friends. He always feeds us exactly what we need to continue the journey; and before he disappears, he leaves on the dinner table a GPS.

New Day

"Waking up this morning, I smile.
Twenty-four brand new hours are before me.
I vow to live fully in each moment
And to look at all being with eyes of compassion."

—Thich Nhat Hanh in *The Heart of the Buddha's Teaching* (Broadway Books, 1998), p. 102.

Richard Rohr in his daily email compares Christians and Buddhists. "Christians are usually talking about metaphysics ('what is') and Buddhists are usually talking about epistemology ('how do we know what is'). In that sense, they offer great gifts to one another." [1]

All I know is that the writings of the Buddhist monk Thich Nhat Hanh so often speak to me. What a marvelous idea to wake up in the morning and say to ourselves, "We have twenty-four brand new hours before us. I don't want to waste a second, a minute, an hour. It is a new day."

Yesterday is past. We went over what we had done and left undone the night before when we prayed that God would forgive us of wrongdoing, also called sins. We remembered where we found joy, often where we least expected it. We recalled where we found love. We remembered the day's experiences in which we saw God working in our life.

This is an extra day, a new beginning. We can no longer regret the past. If we have harmed others, we will make living amends where we need to; but today we are offered a fresh start. We hope we have learned from the past. We will not keep doing the same thing every day and expect different results. We will look for synchronicity or moments or serendipity in which we make connections, see how events are related.

I write about the Eucharist one morning and someone not aware of that confides later that same morning about how important the Eucharist is in his life. We receive a message from a friend we have been thinking about that day. We think about someone we have not seen for some time, and then that person calls. The person tells us that what we did or said was exactly what she needed at the time. That is synchronicity. These are God connections, and they are all around us in each new day.

[1] Richard Rohr, *Center for Action and Contemplation, Meditation: Mindfulness, cac.org*, August 24, 2018.

God's Image

"Within the best of us, there is some evil, and within the worst of us, there is some good. The person who hates you most has some good in him; even the nation who hates you most has some good in it; even the race that hates you most has some good in it. And when you come to the point that you look in the face of every person and see deep down within what religion calls 'the image of God,' you begin to love in spite of. No matter what the person does, you see God's image there."—Martin Luther King, Jr., in "Loving Your Enemies," sermon at Dexter Ave. Baptist Church, Montgomery, Alabama, 1957.

I once worked with another physician, whom I thought incompetent. I thought the decisions she made did not make sense and were not helpful. She often talked almost in riddles, trying to look at many sides of a question—while I already thought there was an obvious answer that, beyond question, was right. She was amazingly slow to make any changes.

Then one weekend I had to do her job when she was on vacation. Overnight I realized why she behaved as she did, the magnitude of her responsibility, and the constant number of real and imagined problems presented to her. I walked in her shoes, and it made all the difference.

Putting myself in her place led me to see God's image in her as well as in so many others I was having difficulty understanding.

A story also circulates that someone asked Mother Teresa the question, "How do you stand it when you have to serve some truly despicable person?" With a sigh, she replies, "I look deeply into their eyes and say to myself, 'My Jesus, what an interesting disguise you are wearing today.'"–Deborah Sokolove, Seekers Church, "Weekly Gospel Reflection," Inward/Outward.com, Church of the Saviour.

Lamott: Prayer

"So prayer is our sometimes real selves trying to communicate with the Real, with Truth, with the Light. It is us reaching out to be heard, hoping to be found by a light and warmth in the world, instead of darkness and cold. Even mushrooms respond to light—I suppose they blink their mushroomy eyes, like the rest of us."
—Anne Lamott in *Help, Thanks, Wow: The Three Essential Prayers* (Hodder & Stoughton, 2001).

When spiritual friends are having difficulty praying, we talk about our present prayer life and what kind of prayer discipline has helped in the past. We discuss the multitude of ways to pray: walking and praying, praying in silence, using prayer books, Ignatian prayers, Centering Prayer, prayer with beads, praying in color, praying the hours.

Anne Lamott's book, *Help, Thanks, Wow,* is a realistic, humorous, short down-to-earth discourse on praying with three subject lines: giving thanks, asking for help, and praising. The book is filled to the brim with simple "one liners" to remember and guide us through the day. One of my favorites is, "If one person is praying for you, buckle up. Things can happen." Another is, "The difference between you and God is that God never thinks he is you." She reminds us that gratitude is not lifting our arms and waving our hands on television but rather picking up trash, doing what is required, reaching out to others in need. When we breathe in gratitude, we breathe it out.

Lamott's section on "Wow" likens that kind of prayer to a child seeing the ocean for the first time. I still remember standing just inside the National Cathedral as a group of fifth graders walked in. I will not forget one small boy who looked up at the high, vaulted gray stone ceilings and exclaimed: "*WOW!*" These are uppercase wows. There are also lower-case wows, such as getting into bed between clean sheets. Lamott suggests that poetry is "the official palace language of *Wow.*" She also reminds us of C. S. Lewis' view of prayer, that we pray not to change God, but to change ourselves.

My experience is that Lamott always stimulates us into new practices of faith or reminds us about those we have forgotten that can make all the difference.

Burton: Life After Death
Guest Writer: Larry Burton

"So, what do you think about life after death?"

As an Episcopal priest, I have heard that question, or others like it, more times than I care to count. I think the Resurrection event may not cover the question of what happens when we die, like I would have thought it did. "But," a friend said, "that was Jesus. This is me." Fair enough.

A group of us have been reading Frederick Buechner's *A Crazy, Holy Grace*. Buechner, now ninety-two, is a prolific author and theologian for whom many of us have great admiration. In part of this book, he imagines a conversation with his beloved grandmother who has been dead for over forty years. She tells him that death is like stepping off a trolley car. Life doesn't stop, but rather continues as a further deepening of understanding of God's grace and love.

That imagined conversation stopped me in my tracks. For most of my life as a theologian I have thought (and taught) something similar, but it was far more abstract, and ultimately not satisfying. Buechner has his grandmother put humanity on my abstractness and offers an image of continuity in God that stopped me flat. Did I believe what I had been teaching? Yes. No question. But now the abstract has taken on a form that both challenges and delights.

So, I had my own conversation with my preacher father and stepmother. Both are dead. But they were delighted to talk with me. "Sorry you had to wait so long to understand," Dad said after I told him about Buechner's book. (My father was a Buechner fan, and so he was way ahead of me.) My stepmother added her two cents' worth: "I always thought suddenly I'd 'get it,' but it didn't happen that way. There are always new layers or new heights, and my heart! My heart just continues to open wider and wider."

My words in their mouths? Or their words in my mouth? Buechner's grandmother challenges her grandson, just as I am challenged. Buechner's major point is that memory can be an astounding portal into the wonders of God. So, what do I think about life after death? I am more convinced than ever that as a beloved child of God, access to the reality of God's love is far more cosmic, mysterious, and wondrous than I had imagined. It is more than Resurrection; it is a continuing transformation, moving toward God's very heart.

Larry Burton
Frederick Buechner's birthday is July 11.

Pickett's Brigade Reunion

"And who is my neighbor?"—Luke 10:29.

Ken Burns' television series on the Civil War describes a remarkable scene that takes place on the fiftieth anniversary of the Battle of Gettysburg, July 3, 1913, when the remainder of the two armies stages a reenactment of Pickett's Charge. The old Union veterans on the ridge take their places among the rocks, and the old Confederate veterans march toward them across the field below—and then something extraordinary happens. As the old men among the rocks rush down at the old men coming across the field, a great cry goes up—except that instead of doing battle, as they had a century earlier, this time they throw their arms around each other and *embrace* and *openly weep*.

In 1914, during World War I, German, British, Belgian, and French troops in the trenches mingled with each other along the western front during a brief Christmas truce and even sang "Silent Night" and other carols in solidarity. Recently we have observed something similar at World War II memorials such as Normandy, where German, English, French, and American soldiers have wept together and shared their stories. We have seen it also when American soldiers return to Vietnam to share stories with those they once bitterly fought against.

This repeated action of shared love and story can tell us something about war. Many of those who have fought on foreign fields can be our strongest advocates against war. They know what they themselves—and those who once were their enemies—have lost. They share a common life-altering experience that only someone who has been there can understand.

Those in recovery of any kind also know how awful their life of obsession was before their healing from addictions to alcohol, drugs, sex, food, etc. They can relate to those who remain trapped in their addiction. Most of all, they can minister to those who are still suffering and offer them hope that their life can be different. They do this by sharing their story of what their life was like in addiction, contrasted to what it is like now in recovery.

Those who have overcome mental illness can become advocates for others who suffer from this common disease. People who were once homeless themselves can offer a restorative hope to those on the street. Cancer survivors can encourage and pray for others recently diagnosed and give them strength and support.

This story goes on and on and on. We are healed as we reach out of ourselves and share our story and listen to sufferers in situations we know all too well. We realize "who IS our neighbor." Some call this becoming wounded healers.

Recognizing God

"He who recognizes a king in disguise treats him differently from he who sees before him only the figure of an ordinary man and treats him accordingly. Likewise, souls who can recognize God in the most trivial, the most grievous and most mortifying things that happen to them, honour everything equally with delight and welcome with open arms what others dread and avoid."—Jean-Pierre de Caussade in *The Sacrament of the Present Moment* (HarperOne, 1966).

I know people like this who seem to treat everyone equally, one person is no more important than another, all are human and divine at the same time. They seem to see the Holy Spirit, the God, the Christ in each person they meet. They do not look merely at the outer appearances or political stature or wealth or power that a person represents. Christ certainly modeled this approach for us.

My experience teaches me that if we cannot see Christ in our neighbor, often it is because we cannot see Christ in ourselves. Consequently, we project onto others our unchristlike behavior that we do not realize is really within us.

How do we change? Along the way, someone comes into our life who treats us as if we really do contain a divine spark, the holy within us—that is, they react to us with love. It is as though a spark becomes lighted. A light, a lightbulb goes on inside of us. We begin to *believe* we are loved.

So, this is our mission as spiritual friends: to seek the light, the Christ in each other.

I remember talking to a spiritual friend about a family member I was having difficulty with. She helped me by asking me, "Tell me something good about her. Something she does well."

My experience also is that I cannot see the Christ in someone else when I live in fear. I realized this recently when attending a meeting at which I was uncomfortable. I wanted to look good. I did not know exactly what they expected of me. I was fearful that I might make a mistake. As an introvert, I did not interact with anyone I did not know. I only had concern for what people might think about me. Was I making a good impression?

At our next meeting, I hope to relate better to others. My plan is, just before the meeting, to say a prayer for each person I know who will be there, asking specifically that we will all see the Christ within each other. I will let you know how it goes.

Ricoeur and Anonymous: May You Live Long Enough
Anonymous Guest Writer

"I find myself only by losing myself"—Paul Ricoeur.

"It is always possible to argue against an interpretation, to confront interpretations, to arbitrate between them and seek for an agreement, even if this agreement remains beyond our reach."—Paul Ricoeur.

May you live long enough...

To laugh at your most embarrassing moments in the past—sportingly owning the temporary title of "dunce"—before passing it on to the next clown in this dance of win-and-lose, hit-and-error called "life."

To side with your own former adversaries, if only for a glancing moment—to accept that in certain past disagreements or outright conflicts that cobble your past: "The other person had a point."

To realize that even your greatest "triumphs" owe much to outside influences: others' kind and diligent contribution, the coming together of circumstances, and "sparks" of grace flung from afar that happened to hit you in the moment.

To experience prayer as the automatic breathing of petitions for others' good—urgently present in your heart before your own needs or requests enter your awareness.

To meet someone whose efforts or example—in any category—put you to "shame," and feel joy that such understanding or expertise or goodness exists in the world apart from your receiving any specific personal gain from it.

To recognize that your "defeats," by the world's judgment, were blessed checks and balances in the larger arc of your journey toward maturity and self-acceptance.

To feel genuinely sad for people who seemed to be unfair and cruel to you for no apparent reason, and to lament the conditions that must have made them that way—even when their cruelty caused you genuine pain.

To let go of any idea that we might be able to judge who is worthy or unworthy of anything that comes to them in this life—or in the life to come.

"We look not at what can be seen but at what cannot be seen; for what can be seen is temporary, but what cannot be seen is eternal." —2 Corinthians 4:18.

"We also boast in our sufferings, knowing that suffering produces endurance, and endurance produces character, and character produces hope, and hope does not disappoint us, because God's love has been poured into our hearts. …"—Romans 5:3-5.

De Mello: *Lectio Divina* and More

"The *meditatio* [meditation part in *Lectio Divina*] is done not with one's mind, but with one's mouth. When the psalmist tells us how he loves to meditate, how he finds it sweeter to his palate than honey from the honeycomb, is he talking about meditation merely as an intellectual exercise? I like to think that he is also talking about the constant recitation of God's law—so he mediates as much with his mouth as with his head."—Anthony de Mello in *Sadhana: A Way to God* (Liguori, 1998).

De Mello also offers a unique method to practice the Benedictine *Lectio Divina*. He suggests we read Scripture (*lectio*) until the word or phrase comes that resonates with us and then stop (*meditatio*) and constantly repeat the word with pauses. In this way, we pray not just with our mind but with our body. When we feel saturated with the word, we stop and enter into prayer (*oratio*). He also suggests a group form of the exercise, using chant along with large segments of silence.

De Mello adds an extra dimension to the Jesus Prayer by imaging Jesus with each word, saying his name with each breath, and finally hearing Jesus call us by name.

De Mello tells the story of the major guilt of a man who just barely misses his father's death. My experience is this so often is an impetus that brings many people to spiritual direction. I am constantly amazed at how God works. We are called back to God even—and maybe even especially—by those who have died.

De Mello calls us to live intimately and fully in the present moment, so to become a part of the grand mystery of God's love for us and for all creation. The present is where we meet God and the present is where spiritual exercises such as Lectio Divina and praying the Jesus prayer take us.

Tangier Island

"'The margins, Nathan,' he said when he started speaking again. 'That's what we're losing. We're losing the churches on the margins. We aren't doing enough for them.'"—Loren Mead to Nathan Kirkpatrick at faithandleadership.com.

Tangier Island is a disappearing island in the Chesapeake Bay, twelve miles equidistant off both the Maryland and the Virginia coast, losing up to sixteen feet of its coastline a year, secondary to the rising sea level from global warming and soil erosion. The government believes that in twenty to thirty years the island will be uninhabitable to the over 500 people who now live there; and in fifty years the island will be completely underwater. The local islanders speak what is described as a unique Elizabethan British-like dialect combined with a southern drawl. They are primarily fishers of oyster and crab, year-round and tourist guides in the summer. The 1.2 square mile island is steeped in religious tradition and actually completely shuts down on Sunday morning.

Nathan Kirkpatrick, writing recently in the *Duke Divinity School Leadership Education Center Alban Weekly* (6/26/2018), recalls the above conversation with the founding director of the Alban Institute, Loren Mead, who compared the Church to Tangier Island. What does Dr. Mead mean by saying the Church is "losing its margins"? Is he saying the Church is shrinking because it is not paying attention to people on the fringes or margins of society—the poor, the weak, the hungry, the homeless, the tired, the sick, those who are the most different from ourselves? In the larger scheme, is he referring to our neighbors who border us that we are not caring about?

I can remember one of my favorite quotes from Bishop Barbara Harris: "The Church is like an oriental rug. Its fringes are what make it most beautiful." In spiritual direction I ask people how the story of Tangier Island might relate to the care of their soul. There are so many possible answers.

Another question is, "Do you ever feel your soul shrinking? Do you feel you are losing the margins, the borders, the uniqueness, the most inspiring and possibly the most interesting parts of your soul, the God, the Christ within you?"

The Art of Being

"In many Muslim cultures, when you want to ask *others* how they're doing, you ask in Arabic, 'how is your *haal?*' In reality, we ask, 'How is your heart doing at this very moment, at this breath?' Tell me you're more than just a machine, checking off items from your to-do list. Put your hand on my arm, look me in the eye, and connect with me for one second. Tell me something about your heart, and awaken my heart."
—Omid Safi in *On Being with Krista Tippett* (9/16/2017).

Omid Safi, Director of Duke University Islamic Studies Center, writes a column on Thursdays for *On Being*. He is teaching us to be more intentional about relationships rather than simply making lists and completing tasks and assignments. My usual greeting to start a conversation is, "How are you doing?" The word *doing* implies that I am interested in what you are *doing*, while I actually want to know how you are *being*—how we can stay connected in this relationship and learn to live together as humans *being* rather than humans *doing*.

Maybe at some point I can say, "How is your heart?" for that sharing is what will make the most difference in allowing us to be in relationship. *Being* implies that we live in the present moment; and it is in the present moment that we connect. My experience is that making eye contact establishes us in the present. If I can hold your hand, we are making physical contact in the present moment.

Can we also transfer this understanding to our relationship to God? Instead of starting our prayers with our *to-do* list for God and expecting God to give us a *to-do* list as well, can we open prayers with

"God, how is your heart? Show me your heart and open up my heart to you."

Harding: Change Again

"But we cannot change anyone else; we can change only ourselves and then usually only when the elements that are in need of reform have become conscious through their reflection in someone else."
—M. Esther Harding.

Esther Harding explains so concisely *how we change.* We often recognize the parts of ourselves that need changing *only as they are reflected in others.* We say, "This is awful. I do not want to be like that." Then, through some unknown factor, perhaps God's Grace, we realize that character defect, that sin, that failing is also in us. I often find myself not wanting to be around a certain person. That is sometimes a clue that he or she is carrying a trait I do not recognize in myself; but seeing it in the other person, I am repulsed by it. The reverse side of this truth is that sometimes the people we most admire carry *a gift* we do not recognize in ourselves.

I also know from 12-step work how people change. They hit bottom. They become so overwhelmed by their condition, so "sick and tired" of how miserable their life is that they will do anything to change.

So, what does all this have to do with our life in the Spirit? My experience is that it is indeed the Spirit, the Christ, the God within us that leads us to change, that whispers in our ear that those defects we acknowledge in others may also be in us—that a better life is possible for us. Those in 12-step programs call it a "moment of clarity." I believe that moment of clarity is God speaking to us; and at that point we find ourselves in a position to listen. Finally, we can hear with "the ear of our heart."

A Letter from Dr. Taybi, a refugee from Iran before he dies

I received this letter from a refugee from Iran, before he died:

Rev. Joanna J. Seibert:

Dear Joanna (please call me Hoosh):

Thank you very much for a very kind email. Your encouragement is most appreciated. I have accepted my illness and have no trouble dealing with the situation, thanks primarily to the support of my loving wife Alice and my children.

I am so thankful for all the opportunities I have been given by my mentors, friends, and many times strangers in this country. Your kindness and reading your email brings me back to 1946, when I was a practicing pediatrician in the city of Hamedan in Iran. An American missionary had a small hospital and clinic headed by a young American, Dr. Frame. I told him one day I was planning to go to America and get more education. A son of a missionary, he spoke Farsi fluently. I told him I wanted to learn *"American."* He taught me a few words in *"American"* [English].

When I left Iran, Mrs. Frame gave a letter to deliver to her parents, the Andersons. I arrived in New York City in December 1948, just before Christmas, and found my way in Manhattan to the Andersons' apartment. Mr. Anderson took me to New York University, met with Professor Tobin, the Dean of Students, and enrolled me in English class. Andersons were missionaries, having spent many years in South America's jungles.

Their kindness did not end here. Many times they invited me to their home, and I spent the 1949 Christmas at their home in New Jersey. The Frames moved back to USA and Dr. Frame had a practice in New York City. It was in 1964 when we gave a course in Pediatric Radiology at Indiana University Medical Center. I sent an invitation for Dr. Frame to come as my guest and attend the course. He could not come. But in a nice note stated: "I see your *'American'* has much improved," referring to my use of *American* instead of *English* in 1948!! This type of kindness is unforgettable. To the end of my life I shall remember what they did for a man from another land and another culture. Two of the Anderson photographs from my album are attached.

I appreciate very much your family remembering meeting this old friend. Please extend my regards to them and I hope we meet again at another SPR gathering.

Hoosh

What I learned from Dr. Taybi

"Before I ventured forth,

even while I was very young,

I sought wisdom openly in my prayer."—Ecclesiasticus 51:13

As I say prayers today for refugees and those trying to immigrate to our country in face of the recent travel ban, I find this note from Dr. Hooshang Taybi from 2006 that was in yesterday's reading. Dr. Taybi wrote the letter three weeks before he died in response to my note about the news of his terminal illness. If you are a radiologist or a pediatrician, you will remember Dr. Taybi, best known for his study of children with difficulties that become part of a syndrome. He was professionally acclaimed for his encyclopedic memory of over 100 journals he read leading to his classic textbook, *The Radiology of Syndromes;* but what I most remember is his kindness, humbleness, and caring for others, empowering others, never too important to spend time with you.

A colleague shares a phrase from Dr. Taybi's favorite Persian poem, "The best way to show your gratitude for having a strong arm is to extend a helping hand to the weak."[1]

I see a life of a brilliant man who close to his death still expresses gratitude for those who helped him over 50 years before. Dr. Taybi empowers us still today by telling stories, stories of children with illnesses, stories of how he was empowered, gratitude for all who touched his life even to the end. I continue to see daily the difference gratitude can make in a person's life. Today I will try to remember and give thanks for those who empowered me and pray that I can pass empowerment and gratitude on to others. I also want to remember Dr. Taybi's story of what a difference the strangers who helped him made in his life. I hope to do this for those who come to our country like Dr. Taybi for a new life.

I also remember that if the present immigration travel ban had been in place, Dr. Taybi would never have come to his America. I think of all of us whose lives would not have been touched by his, but especially the children and their parents who would have missed his medical expertise.

[1]Ron Cohen, Charles Gooding, "Memorial Hooshang Taybi," in *AJR*, 187:1382-1383, 2006.

Hyde: Dreams 1

Guest Writer Bridget Hyde

"What I have continued to find… is that dreams are sources of wisdom for problem solving and life enhancement. They put us in touch with dimensions of ourselves that are normally hidden and that we need in order to grow toward our full potential."—George R. Slater in *Bringing Dreams to Life* (Paulist Press, 1995).

Dreams are a very dynamic form of spiritual direction. They come to us in the service of wholeness. A visit from a dream brings unconscious information to our consciousness. Dreams carry a divine desire to make us whole, to integrate the conscious and unconscious worlds and find a balance between soul and persona.

There is much talk in spiritual direction about "ego" and how it keeps us from God, from our truest self. My experience has taught me that ego is not in and of itself bad. It is an ego out of balance that harms.

Don't we all need egos for our basic needs? It is our ego that drives us to get dressed and go out into the world. My faith tells me that God gave us our egos so we might have the confidence to put forward our gifts, and accomplish necessary, daily tasks. Sadly, some of us fall into situations here on earth that sap the vitality of our egos, our self-esteem. During dark or denigrating times, people often dream of kings and queens. Here, the dream seeks to balance a personal sense of worth by calling forth a regal, powerful archetype.

When an ego is out of balance the other way, it becomes inflated and sees itself above others, immune from harm or

wrongdoing. If this happens to a person, the unconscious will sometimes bring a dream of falling from a high place to land on solid ground. The dream will seek to bring the person "back to earth." Thus, a person may have a dream that a plane crashes, yet they land safely somehow; or another example is a dream where a car stalls and the dreamer must get out and walk. The major thrust of such dreams is to help the dreamer feel grounded, to avoid the fate of Icarus.
—Bridget Hyde

Hyde: Dreams 2
Guest Writer Bridget Hyde

"What I have continued to find…is that dreams are sources of wisdom for problem solving and life enhancement. They put us in touch with dimensions of ourselves that are normally hidden and that we need in order to grow toward our full potential."—George R. Slater in *Bringing Dreams to Life* (Paulist Press, 1995).

The first dream that I took to spiritual direction was a dream about walking barefoot in the snow. When my foot touched the ground in the dream, I became aware that I was dreaming, and then I started to pray. Now, as I reflect on that dream, I see a person who is becoming conscious of the divine nature of dreams. When my bare foot touched the ground, I became grounded in the grace of the unconscious.

I had been recording my dreams, sharing them with friends, and honoring them with symbol work, but I had not sought discernment in this work from a spiritual director. When I told a friend this dream, she begged me to work on the dream with a retired Episcopal priest and spiritual director named Allen Whitman. I followed her stern invitation and began a five-year study of my dreams with Allen. From this inward study, I became aware of many different aspects of my character. My work in dreams began to show me how to connect the symbolic language of a dream to the circumstances of my life. For example, during a time when I was making a big decision, I had a dream that my airline flight was interrupted. The dream plane was grounded, and I was forced to wait before boarding another plane.

When Allen and I worked on the dream, we both realized that I had come to a time of waiting in the decision process. Because of this dream, I waited to take decisive actions. I am so glad I did. It was a wonder to see my work in dreams as a kind of spiritual direction. I started to trust my dreams and their divine nature. Looking back, I see how God has guided me through my dreams, and I honor spiritual direction in dreams as a holy gift.

—Bridget Hyde

Grisham: Ignatian Method of Discernment, Peace of God
Guest Writer Lowell Grisham

No one has done more work on the discipline of discernment than the Jesuits, the monastic descendants of Ignatius of Loyola. Although I can't recall who taught it to me, for many years I've used an Ignatian discernment method from time to time when I've faced a choice between two options. Here's the way it was given to me:

In a battle in the early 1500s, Ignatius was seriously wounded. (I believe an artillery shell shattered his leg.) He spent months of painful convalescence. He found that his pain was relieved sometimes when he would go into periods of *active imagination*. He imagined what his life would be like when he was healed and released from the hospital. He made up stories about his future life, using all of his senses to place himself into the future. He created scenes from his imagined future and experienced them vividly—with sight, sound, touch, taste, and smell—thinking and feeling what his alternative life might be.

Whenever Ignatius was actively imagining, his pain would decrease, and the time seemed to pass more quickly. He discovered that his imagination gravitated toward *two narratives*. In one narrative, he would experience himself becoming a great, chivalrous knight, doing valiant deeds of courage and winning the hand of a noble maiden. In the other narrative, he would experience himself becoming a knight for Christ, boldly taking the gospel into the most remote or challenging or needed places. While in active imagination, Ignatius experienced relief with either narrative. But he noticed a significant difference about where his spirit went *afterwards,* when he was just taking care of business in a normal state of consciousness.

He noticed in the hours following his narratives about becoming a noble warrior knight, that he experienced a sense of turbulence, discomfort, and even desolation. But he noticed in the hours following his imagining about becoming a knight for Christ, that he experienced a sense of consolation, harmony, and especially *peace.* Ignatius interpreted the sense of peace to be the presence of God, drawing him into God's will for him, helping him to discern the direction of his future. He embraced the vision of that second narrative, and became a noble knight for Christ, desiring to undertake the greatest service possible to the Church and the world.

The presence of *peace* is a sign of God's will. In the chaos and storm of a decision, when there are two potential options or directions, I will sometimes use a form of Ignatian discernment practice. I'll set before me the *two options. One day* I will spend some time actively imagining myself living into the first option, using all five senses to create scenes from that future possibility. Then I will go about my normal daily activity, but I'll keep a bit of attention directed to notice where my spirit goes. *Another day,* I'll spend time in active imagination living into the other option. Then I will pay attention to my spirit, mood, and intuition during ordinary business. What after-effect is there following each separate scenario?

If I sense some form of consolation and peace in the ordinary time following active imagination with one narrative, and if I sense turbulence in the ordinary time following imagination with the other narrative, I'll accept that as a sign of God's will. The presence of *peace* is key.

Where does the peace of Christ lead us, especially when our boat seems tossed and we've lost control of our direction? A sense of peace can give direction toward God's will for us and for the fullest exercise of our creativity, courage, freedom, and service. Sometimes a little active imagination can lead us toward discernment.

—Lowell Grisham

When someone comes for a visit for discernment, this is what I first offer. It was loaned to me by Lowell Grisham, retired Rector of St. Paul's Episcopal Church, Fayetteville, Arkansas.

Kanuga Chapel

"The God who existed before any religion counts on you to make the oneness of the human family known and celebrated."—Archbishop Desmond Tutu.

The Chapel of Transfiguration at Kanuga Conference Center in North Carolina has always been a place where the family of God is celebrated in so many ways. I love the outer and inner appearance of the chapel, made of southern Carolina white pine from trees downed in a severe storm in 1936.

My mind always wanders as I sit in the chapel waiting for any service to begin, and I remember more. The wood for the chapel was not pretreated, so there are these unusual dark oval markings on the wood, left by the oiled fingerprints of the workers. The simple prints are more prominent on the ceiling, where it was more difficult for the builders to work.

When I am in the chapel, I feel surrounded not only by the thousands of prayers of people on retreat who have worshiped here, but also by the hands of those who labored on the building.
I remember about our own fingerprints and where we leave them, as well as the fingerprints of others and where we have been touched by theirs.

I especially remember the day sitting in the chapel when I had just found out that my fingerprints for my TSA Pre-check did not go through strongly enough. That meant the FBI would investigate me before I got my Pre-check, which would delay my receiving my traveler number! This is the identification you carry to go through a special security lane at airports. It allows you to avoid taking off your shoes or coat or putting your laptop out separately. I walk with a cane and have special long lace-up shoes that are difficult to take off and on; so, getting my traveler number is significant for me.

I have a new appreciation for the builders of this chapel, who must have been so much stronger and would have been tightly holding onto the wood in order to leave their prints in this sacred space.

I remember other services in this chapel I wanted never to end. I have memories from a preaching conference, dancing around the altar with Barbara Brown Taylor as I offered the bread, and she followed with the wine. I see Bishop Tutu dancing on the green after an amazing closing Eucharist at a retreat led by Trinity Wall Street. Priceless. I remember two Lenten retreats where we were snowed in. Breathtaking.

I played my harp at one retreat that Phyllis Tickle led in this chapel because the scheduled musicians could not get here; and I played at the closing of our spiritual direction class at the Hayden Institute. A privilege.

Thin places like Kanuga can offer us a full album of memories to go back to and remember times when God's presence and love were immanently present—or, as Gordon Cosby would tell us, times when we lived in the real world.

Miracles

"A cancer inexplicably cured. A voice in a dream. It is possible to look at most miracles and find a rational explanation in terms of natural cause and effect. It is possible to look at Rembrandt's *Supper at Emmaus* and find a rational explanation in terms of paint and canvas."—Frederick Buechner in *Beyond Words* (HarperOne, 2009).

I believe in miracles. Once a week I step into a room full of people who are themselves miracles. It is a 12-step recovery group of people who once were crippled by an addiction and now are "happy, joyous and free." They talk about what it was like then and what it is like now. I have heard some of their stories hundreds of times; but each time I see a few more similarities to my own story and identify more closely with theirs. Sometimes a person's story is so similar to mine that I think: *That IS* my story. The differences blur. Everyone in the room is a miracle, and I realize that I am as well. And so, each time, I leave that place profoundly grateful.

I see other miracles every day. Someone calls or comes for a visit. I just listen and listen. In my mind, I have no idea what to say. Sometimes words come out of my mouth that seem to help my friend. I am in the dark as to where a particular idea might have come from. I know that its flashing into my mind was a miracle not of my own making. Some would call it the Spirit working in our lives.

I see people living for many years through cancers that in the past would have killed them in months. These are all miracles. People who find cures are miracle workers. Often they are inspired by seeing patients die of a certain disease and are determined not to experience that again.

I remember a conversation with my grandmother when I was a junior in medical school and we were riding together in the back seat of a car. She told me she could not understand how people do not believe in miracles when they see a newborn baby. I just smiled, but in my mind I was thinking: "Grandmother, I know how babies develop. I know all the secrets and the stages of how they come to be born. These are all facts of science."

Now, fifty years later, as I have seen so many sick newborns, I know my grandmother is right. The birth of every baby is a miracle.

I also know what Buechner is talking about when we see Rembrandt's *Supper at Emmaus* at the Louvre in Paris. Rembrandt has captured the miracle. So many other works of art qualify as miracles as well. They connect us to the God of our understanding: Rembrandt's *Return of the Prodigal Son* at the Hermitage Museum in St. Petersburg; Caravaggio's *Supper at Emmaus* in the National Gallery in London; Georges de La Tour's *The Repentant Magdalen* at the National Gallery in Washington, D. C.

Buechner challenges us to remember the many works of art that speak individually to us and to look at them anew. Do we recognize the miracles offered to us in art books—or even better, might we plan a pilgrimage to go see these masterpieces for ourselves as we learn more about the miracles in them and ourselves?

Early Riser

"Wisdom is radiant and unfading,
and she is easily discerned by those who love her,
and is found by those who seek her.
She hastens to make herself known to those who desire her.
One who rises early to seek her will have no difficulty,
for she will be found sitting at the gate."—Wisdom 6:12-14.

Many of the spiritual friends I know are early risers. Early morning is their time to read or meditate or write before the business of the day begins. I used to walk around our neighborhood in the early morning before going to the hospital to work. Now I look out of a floor to ceiling picture window and watch and wait for the sun to come up and the cardinals and blue jays and woodpeckers to appear at my feeder.

At the beach, I like to sit outside and feel night becoming day. I like to feel the Gulf breeze and watch the water creatures gather to begin their day. This is their home. They are local. I am a visitor. The lone osprey circles high above the waves. The single blue heron swoops in and slowly struts on his stilts to be as near as possible to the early morning fishermen at the edge of the Gulf, hoping he will receive their small rejections. The pelicans fly in military formation, so close to the waves that they must constantly get their feathers wet.

The early risers are like the women at the empty tomb on Easter morning. They are seeking resurrection, a new beginning— and they will find it every day as the sun majestically rises above the horizon with its color guard, especially on Sunday mornings.

Johnson: Inner Work

"All forms of interaction with the unconscious that nourished our ancestors—dream, vision, ritual, religious experience—are largely lost, dismissed by the modern mind as primitive or superstitious. In our hubris, our faith in our unassailable reason, cuts ourselves off from our origins in the unconscious and from the deepest parts of ourselves."—Robert Johnson in *Inner Work: Using Dreams and Active Imagination for Personal Growth* (Harper & Row, 1989).

My spiritual director posted this quote on Facebook today. It is an affirmation for an alternative path that a group of us are beginning again. Our book group is rereading the revised version of Joyce Rockwood Hudson's *Natural Spirituality*. We recently were in a clergy group and announced that we were studying *Natural Spirituality*. Two members who had recently finished seminary had no idea what we were talking about. When we mentioned dream work, they were even more in the dark, and maybe a little suspicious. Older clergy in the group had been studying dreams for some time and affirmed the value of the study.

I have been involved in dream groups on and off for over thirty years. Dream work is one of the many ways to discern what God is calling us to do in our lives. My experience is that it is important to participate in a group of people studying their own and each other's dreams. Most of us find it difficult to discern dreams by ourselves.

There are many factors to consider. Dreams tell us something we don't already know. Parts of ourselves may block fresh information. Think of our experience in other discussion groups when novel ideas come up. There is invariably at least one person who flings out an automatic "no" to an alternative way of doing things. "That is not the way we have done it in the past."

It always takes time for the entire group to process the information and decide to go in a new direction. Likewise, a dream group of friends looking at a dream from outside of our own ego may gently guide us in a new direction that the automatic "no" part of us might have shut down. We look for these insights into our inner life until the light bulb turns on inside and outside of us. I like Joyce Rockwood Hudson's subtitle of her book, *A Handbook for Jungian Inner Work in Spiritual Community*.

De Mello: Out of the Head

"The head is not a very good place for prayer. It is not a bad place for *starting* your prayer. But if your prayer stays there too long and doesn't move into the heart, it will gradually dry up and prove tiresome and frustrating."—Anthony de Mello in *Sadhana: A Way to God* (Liguori, 1998).

Anthony de Mello's *Sadhana: A Way to God* is an amazing book—a collection of "one of a kind, practical spiritual exercises" blending Eastern and Western spiritual practice for contemplative prayer. De Mello describes contemplative prayer as communicating with God with a minimal use of words. He lists forty-seven exercises, all of which can be learned through practicing each for a week at a time.

In his first section, de Mello repeatedly teaches about how contemplative prayer comes after achieving an awareness—awareness of the body, not just the mind; and awareness of God's presence.

The second section is about using fantasy in prayer; and the last section is on employing devotion in contemplative prayer. The awareness exercises especially help us get out of our head and into our bodies—where de Mello says we must return to our senses. He describes the head as a place to begin to pray; but becoming aware of the feelings in our entire body, paying attention to our breath, and returning to our senses keeps us in the present presence. It is in the present moment that God meets us—not where we are anticipating or dreading the future or resenting or gloating over the past, but in the now. Our head lives in the past or the future. Our body, our heart, grounds us to the present moment.

Spiritual Practice of Fishing

"If, then, I were asked for the most important advice I could give, that which I considered to be the most useful to the men of our century, I should simply say: in the name of God, stop a moment, cease your work, look around you."—Leo Tolstoy in *Essays, Letters, and Miscellanies* (Scribner's, 1929).

I sit outside each early morning on the Gulf Coast just after sunrise and watch lone surf fishermen come like clockwork to the water's edge with their fishing rods, fishing rod holders, buckets, bait, and folding beach chairs. They are early risers, arriving before the pelicans and seagulls and dolphins come out of hiding. The members of this all-male club mark their territory as they spike two rod holders into the sand as the only signs of human presence. They unfold their chairs, bait their lines, cast them beyond the roaring, white ocean's surf, and sit and wait between the two holders for the rods to jump and bend.

The nibbles are infrequent, so they spend most of the time sitting and staring out into the Gulf. They peer out as if they can see all the way beyond South America. They do not take out their cell phones or read books. They wait patiently, usually for several hours, presumably with great faith that their efforts will connect them to the gift of unknown food from beneath the sea.

I have become so fascinated in watching the fishermen that I recognize them by their walk, what they are wearing, whom they talk to, what time they come out, and how long they stay. When I have talked to them, they have taught me much about spirituality and faithfulness and how to surrender to a spiritual practice. Indeed, some of the fishermen refer to their daily routine as a spiritual practice; while others would be appalled at giving their fishing exercise such a name. They all agree that this recreational sport brings them peace; and most realize that it is not fish that they are after. It is re-creation.

Perhaps this uncertainty girded by faith is also part of our spiritual practices: Centering Prayer, saying the Rosary, walking the labyrinth, praying, fasting, *lectio divina*, worshiping. The peace comes in the offering of time, a piece of our life, to the practice, rather than always reaching any goal or making or receiving a connection.

My second gift from our fishermen is that in spending time observing them I have stayed grounded, connected to my surroundings, living in the present moment. The fishermen are teaching me about looking out beyond the turbulent water's edge and having faith that there is something greater than any of us that is constantly trying to connect to us.

Enneagram

"In the study of personality, the Enneagram is designed for self-inquiry. By discovering one's Enneagrammic personality, one comes to know the many layers of self in a personal and particular way. The Enneagram points out how a person's strengths can become more stable and more dynamic, and how weaknesses can be brought to consciousness and even healed."—Joseph Howell in *Becoming Conscious: The Enneagram's Forgotten Passageway* (Balboa Press, 2012).

We recently spent a weekend at an Enneagram conference led by Dr. Howell at Kanuga. This nine-point ancient study of the personality can be helpful not only by teaching us about ourselves and our strengths, but in the healing of wounds that led to our forming certain personality traits. The Enneagram can also help us learn to become compassionate with ourselves and with others of different personality types.

On the Enneagram, I am a two, the helper, with a strong three wing, the achiever. My other wing, the four, the creative type, can lead me to the source of my basic essence or God within. That may explain why I am writing this daily message about spiritual direction and spiritual practices.

At the conference, there were nine tables where people could go and talk to others who shared one of the nine personality types. I immediately identified with the twos' table. I heard the music in my mind and in my body from "Going Home," the theme from Dvorak's Largo in his *New World Symphony*. I was with a group of people who knew me and I knew them. I could see their woundedness and I could easily recognize their soul, the God in them.

If a person comes to spiritual direction who has had some experience with the Enneagram, I try to help that person see God, the soul within—for this is what the ancient practice is all about.

Rebecca Spooner lead an Enneagram Retreat at St. Mark's Episcopal Church, Little Rock, Saturday, February 29, 2020 that was so helpful. This was one of the last things we did before the pandemic changed our lives. It seems so long ago. Today I will review what Rebecca taught us to remember a different outside world and how it affected our inner world.

Thurman: Love from My Heart

"I want to be more loving in my heart! It is often easy to see it with my mind, and give assent to the thought of being loving. But I want to be more loving in my heart! So I must ease the tension in my heart that ejects the sharp barb, the stinging word. I want to be more loving in my heart so that, through both unconscious awareness and deliberate intent, I shall be a kind, gracious human being. I want to be more loving in my heart!"—Howard Thurman.

Howard Thurman was an African American theologian and educator who considerably influenced Martin Luther King, Jr., in the theology of racial nonviolence in our last century. I read into this quote that Dr. Thurman is actually praying to connect to love, to the Christ, the divine, within himself. I also hear the difficulty he may have "ejecting the sharp barb." We can be comforted in knowing that this prominent proponent of nonviolence knows it is not a straightforward task. He is praying that when we connect to this love, the divine within, that we will love others and "be a kind and gracious human being" consciously as well as unconsciously.

Dr. Thurman is reminding us that when we are living in connection with the Holy Spirit, the divine within us, we will know the fruit of the Spirit, "love, joy, peace, patience, kindness, generosity, faithfulness, gentleness, and self-control" (Galatians 5:22-23). But how do we get there? This is the calling of every spiritual practice: meditation, prayer, reading, corporate worship, fasting, and so many others, to put ourselves in position to connect to God within.

Perhaps if Paul were writing today he might have told his scribe to use the word "nonviolence" as one of the fruit of the Spirit, even though it is already so loudly speaking out in all the other fruit of the Spirit.

I pray that Dr. Thurman is still praying for us today to learn to "love from our hearts" in these times when the message of nonviolence is so needed.

Ezekiel: Shower Chant

"I will sprinkle clean water upon you, and you shall be clean from all your uncleanness. A new heart I will give you, and a new spirit I will put within you; and I will remove from your body the heart of stone and give you a heart of flesh. I will put my spirit within you."—Ezekiel 36:25-27a.

I am up early watching light come today as a gentle rain sounds outside my window and on our roof. I can imagine this rain cleansing our planet as well as my heart. Maybe later I will have the courage to go outside and stand or sit and feel the rain on my face, hair, and clothes and pray for a heart of flesh instead of stone, for just this day.

One of the first priests I worked with when I was a deacon in training shared with me that he chanted these few verses from Ezekiel in his shower each morning. I think of and pray for him each time I recite these words, which are now one of the alternative Canticles in Morning Prayer in *Enriching our Worship I* (Church Publishing, 1998).

As I talk with spiritual friends who confide concerns about the heart of stone they carry, I also let them know that I suffer from the same dis-ease. My experience is that our responsibility is to recover an awareness of *when we cannot feel the Spirit within us and our hearts turn to stone.* Awareness is a major gift that God calls us to develop and discern. Only God can change our heart. We keep that prayer to be open to change in our hearts every day. We try to put ourselves in relationship to others who also desire a heart of flesh and not of stone, and we pray for each other.

The Righteous Gentiles of World War II, July 16

"Lord of the Exodus, who delivers your people with a strong hand and a mighty arm: Strengthen your Church with the examples of the righteous Gentiles of World War II to defy oppression for the rescue of the innocent; through Jesus Christ."—Collect of the Day: The Righteous Gentiles, July 16, in *Holy Women, Holy Men, Celebrating the Saints* (Church Publishing, 2010) and in *A Great Cloud of Witnesses* (Church Publishing, 2016).

Holy Women, Holy Men is a trial expanded calendar of commemorations of saints authorized by the 2009 General Convention of the Episcopal Church that includes many modern people of faith and apostolic action. The people remembered on July 16 are the thousands of Christians and people of faith who saved Jews from the Holocaust. One of them was Carl Lutz, an Evangelical Christian who was a Swiss Vice-Council in Budapest. Lutz negotiated with the Nazis for the deportation of over 60,000 Jews to Palestine, probably saving more lives than any other person.

Lutz had gained permission to issue emigration papers for 8,000 Jews to Palestine. He interpreted it as applicable for 8,000 families, saving thousands more. There is a 2014 American film, *Walking with the Enemy,* that tells of Lutz's work with Pinchas Rosenbaum in Budapest during the German occupation of Hungry. Lutz also established seventy-six safe houses in which to hide Jews in Budapest, including the now famous Glass House, all of which the diplomat declared as Swiss territory.

There is another documentary about Lutz called *The Forgotten Hero*. I honestly believe each of us is given many moments in which to make a difference in the lives of others. The challenges may not be as dangerous or risky as Lutz's on the international scene; but in our own environment they may still demand courage. It is good for us to see how people who came before us were creative in making changes and finding loopholes when there seemed to be no way out—as they worked around systems that were awful beyond words. I can only believe this was the work of the Holy Spirit in the worst of times. I know that same Holy Spirit is working in us today.

Carl Lutz, International Raoul Wallenberg Foundation, www.raoulwallenberg.net.

Psalm 23 and Who Are the Shepherds?

"The Lord is my shepherd."—Psalm 23.

Malinda Elizabeth Berry reminds us in an article, "Who Is My Shepherd?" in ChristianCentury.org (7/19/2018) of a frequent misconception about the gender of shepherds. In biblical times, shepherding was often carried out by young girls as well as boys and men. Berry reminds us that beautiful Rachel was tending her father Laban's sheep when Jacob first saw her and fell in love with her (Genesis 29:9-10). Zipporah and her sisters were trying to water their father's sheep when Moses drove away some other shepherds who were bothering them (Exodus 2:16-17).

We may also infer from this that these young and fair maidens were just as masterful with a slingshot as young David!

Berry asks us if we have ever seen any Bible story pictures or paintings with girls as shepherds. Indeed, I could only find a few, including one by Hungarian painter Marko Andrea (1887) called *Shepherd Girl.* Berry then challenges us to consider having girls as well as boys dress up as shepherds in this year's Christmas pageant! (At our staff meeting, Luke, our Family Ministries Coordinator at St. Mark's, reminded me that, unknown to me, St. Mark's has been including girl shepherds for years!)

For me, this is one more example of a tradition that doesn't ring true with the historical facts: that shepherds should be only boys or men. It makes me wonder why I didn't think of girls as shepherds even after having read the stories of Rachel and Zipporah more times than I can remember. Now it is so obvious.

I hope you can share my excitement with Berry's fresh information about stories we thought we knew so well. It reminds us not to gloss over old Bible stories, but rather to hope to see new insights each time we read them. This also encourages us to keep researching what others are discovering in their study of the Bible. It is a reminder that the Holy Spirit is alive and well and continually teaching us new insights from old stories.

Wisdom of Children

"The wolf shall live with the lamb,
  the leopard shall lie down with the kid,
the calf and the lion and the fatling together,
  and a little child shall lead them."—Isaiah 11:6

There are so many stories in the Bible about the wisdom and leadership of children and youth. An adolescent boy leads Saul to Samuel (1 Samuel 9). Baby Moses' sister Miriam keeps watch over him until Pharaoh's daughter finds him and suggests a "nurse" for him (Exodus 2:1-10). A young captured Israelite girl tells Naaman's wife about Elisha, who can cure his leprosy (2 Kings 5). In the Gospel of John, Andrew brings a young boy with five barley loaves and two small fish to Jesus to feed five thousand people (John 6:1-14). I know there are more stories. Help me remember them.

As a physician for children, and now a grandmother, the importance of children has daily become so evident to me. Children teach me about joy. They model awareness. They show me how to live in the moment. Their connection to the sacred seems to be on a shorter string than mine.

As a parent, I was so worried about raising my children "right" that I often missed their wisdom as they were growing up. I do remember one time I listened to my young daughter and stopped my busy work to go outside to see the rainbows in our lawn sprinkler—after she came running in to tell me about all the rainbows outside.

My grandchildren are growing up too fast. Our oldest is now in her second year of college. I do not want to miss a second I might have with any of them.

I also loved being a part of the Cathedral School when I was at Trinity Cathedral. I am now assigned as a deacon to St. Mark's, where there is a Day School. I cherish every opportunity I can get to spend time with these preschoolers. I love the way they fold their tiny hands and kneel to pray in chapel. Sometimes their heads are bowed. Sometimes they look up with wonder, seeking to "get" what this new adventure is all about. They teach me more each day about God and God's love than most of the books on my bookshelf, as they share their connection to God.

So, when people come to me for spiritual direction, I always recommend spending time with children, especially one on one, to learn more about God's love. Barbara Brown Taylor suggests getting down on the floor with them. I can no longer do that; but I can still sit and listen to their stories and share meals with them and throw kisses and give hugs. I also love to watch movies with them and remind them every time I see them that *we love them and they are beautiful inside and out.*

Feeding, Being Fed

"The question of bread for myself is a material question, but the question of bread for my neighbor is a spiritual question."—Nikolai Berdyaev.

Certainly, Jesus gives us continued examples of his feeding thousands as well as going to eat at the home of others, often with the most despised such as Zacchaeus and Matthew, tax collectors. Jesus, a role model in this, feeds others and lets others feed him. For Christians, Jesus leaves us with another meal, the Eucharist of bread and wine, a sacrament reminding us of his care and bringing his presence to us.

When I am having difficulty with someone, I imagine us together at the altar rail, kneeling, if possible, to receive the bread and the wine of the Eucharist. Jesus is with us. After kneeling together, I see the person in a different light. Sometimes I can see the Christ within him or her.

I have given up trying to understand why eating a meal with someone else can help us develop a relationship faster than spending hours talking to that person. As we are being fed, we see the person more clearly. Often we can carry on a deeper conversation when food is present. It is almost as if the food is a natural ice breaker.

I remember when, in my medical practice, I worked with nine other physicians. Each of them had unique gifts and were advocates for distinct parts of our practice. Each person wanted his or her area to be funded and fully staffed.

One day we decided to have lunch together once a week to try to work through difficult issues. The situation changed almost overnight. We began to see each other's needs as they related to our many areas of interest. We prioritized what was really most important for the patients we were caring for, instead of focusing on our own needs. Some of us even became lifelong friends!

Flexible Bible

"Mary Cosby used to begin her New Testament class by bending her soft-cover Bible and saying she preferred a Bible that was flexible. Then she would say, 'The Bible is not a manual for morality, but a mirror for identity.'"—Carol Martin, Bread of Life Church, "A Mirror for Identity" at InwardOutward.org, Church of the Saviour, July 15, 2018.

My first introduction to this deeper and more flexible Bible study was with a small group of people at St. Mark's in Little Rock in the 1980s with a leader named Dick Moore in a room above the children's classrooms that we called "the upper room." As we studied the books of the Bible, Dick reminded us that the Bible was a roadmap, not the destination.

I think of old friends like Carole and Gary Kimmel who were in our class who now live on the Outer Banks in North Carolina. I remember Betty and Brady Anderson, who went on to be Bible translators in Africa in Tanzania, and how Brady later became the American Ambassador to that country. They taught me so much. Together we uncovered new insights from the Bible that had never before occurred to us.

As we saw God present in the lives of people in the Bible who were just like us—with gifts and faults—we also became more aware of God, the Holy Spirit, at work in our own and others' lives. We saw that the relationship of the Holy Spirit did not end with first- and second-century Christians; rather, the Spirit is still leading us today. If we believe only a strict, literal translation of the Bible, we are denying the continued presence of the Holy Spirit working in our lives today and ever bringing us more good news.

I am thinking of the Bible I received from my Bishop nineteen years ago at my ordination. It, as well, is flexible.

Schmidt: *Dys-Feng Shui* 1
Guest Writer Frederick Schmidt

"To believe in something, and not to live it, is dishonest."—Mahatma Gandhi.

I don't know a great deal about *feng shui* (pronounced *fung shwee),* but it is, as I understand it, a Chinese concept of aesthetics that applies "the laws of heaven and earth" to create harmony and order. It teaches how to maximize the use of life's energy in order to be in sync with the world around us.

Today it is used in a rather more trivialized and commercial fashion by interior decorators who probably don't know a lot about ancient Chinese philosophy. But they know an exotic way to sell their services when they see one!

In the middle of a rather lengthy business meeting some years ago, those of us around the table found a way to kill a few free moments by joking about the rather strange table arrangement we had been given for our meeting. The worst of it was that there were people sitting at tables behind us. They were forced to face the backs of our heads, and we were positioned with our backs to them.

Thus, one of the funnier "you had to be there to understand" moments was the one in which we critiqued the arrangement as a product of *"dys-feng shui."*

Whether you find that funny or not, I think it is true that the more we live into the spiritual life, the more we take responsibility for the world around us. We notice *feng shui* and *dys-feng shui*—or to turn the vocabulary in a direction that is a bit more familiar to me; we notice where the Spirit of God is at work and where the Spirit of God is marginalized.

I am not talking about some kind of soft social consciousness, never mind a body of political beliefs. I am referring to the capacity to look at the world around us through the eyes of God.

Frederick Schmidt

Schmidt: *Feng Shui* 2
Guest Writer Frederick Schmidt

"Whenever you are creating beauty around you, you are restoring your own soul."—Alice Walker.

Not everyone who identifies as spiritual necessarily takes that larger responsibility into consideration. In fact, most of us are taught that spirituality is about getting God involved in our lives, fixing our problems, comforting us when we are down, showing us the way. Our culture has taught us to think that way; and some spiritualities are devoted to that understanding of the spiritual life.

Now, at one level, I'm all for God being involved in my life. I don't relish having problems. When God seems particularly close, I enjoy the palpable sense of peace that goes along with such moments, and I never mind knowing what to do next. But, at the same time, I don't think that is the purpose of the spiritual life.

We have a larger responsibility. *Feng shui* doesn't quite capture that responsibility, but it hints at a concept found in the Torah, in the prophets, and in the teaching of Jesus—pretty much in the entire Bible, in fact. It's called the righteousness of God—the order God intended, to put it in more accessible terms. Put another way, we are called into partnership with Jesus to care about the way how the world around us does or does not conform to God's design.

Contributing to the righteousness of God won't be as easy as rearranging the furniture in a room. Doing that in our world is a much bigger job. Not everyone will think that God's opinion on where the furniture should go will agree with us where it should be all the time. And this side of eternity, the furniture will never be where all of it should be.

But we can witness to making God's righteousness a reality. We can make personal choices and relate to one another in ways that reflect the presence of God in our lives. Those may not be sizeable pieces of furniture, but it's a good place to start.

Frederick Schmidt

Charleston: Feminine Spirit

"There is no power men can devise that can overcome the strength, dignity, and courage of women. Trying to deny the rights of women is like trying to outlaw life itself. The Spirit that stands by her sisters stands eternal. The Mother that defends her daughters never sleeps."—Bishop Steven Charleston, Daily Facebook Page.

I remember when I first encountered the feminine Spirit of the God of my understanding. It was in the 1980s. I became acutely aware of the masculine slant of the words and works of the liturgy and practices of my tradition. There was no honoring of the feminine in language or in church practices. I tried changing pronouns in the service, and that worked for a while.

The altar party was made up of men. I longed to worship with other women, maybe even—heaven forbid—around an altar. So we started a group on Saturday mornings using our church facility to study and learn about feminine spirituality. We soon had a huge crowd. How comforting to know that others were hungry for this facet of the divine.

After a couple of years, as more women from very different traditions joined the group, the words and practices became even too radical for me. I knew I had to make a decision: remain in my tradition and wait for changes; or go over to join in practices now were in territories too foreign for me.

I decided to stay with my tradition. Soon I saw improvements there. Our Prayer Book changed by adopting less masculine language. Women were given much greater roles in the Church.

I know and believe in the feminine Spirit of God that Bishop Charleston is talking about. It is a power that visited my mind and body and spirit when I least expected it; and for some time, I could not understand it. I had been living in the very masculine world of medicine at the time. Suddenly I saw a unique way of looking at things, of working out problems, of relating to others, of worshiping and honoring and praising God.

Why I was awakened by this power, I do not know. It was like a Damascus Road experience. I had no choice but to pursue it. It was like experiencing another pregnancy. Perhaps this nudge came from one of my deceased grandmothers who lived under a masculine rule, but subtly tried to accomplish something different. I know only that my job now is to treasure the gift of the feminine spirit and to pass on or model the gift for my children and grandchildren. I know it can change the world just as it changed me.

Nature

"Everybody needs beauty as well as bread, places to play in and pray in, where Nature may heal and cheer and give strength to body and soul alike."—John Muir.

A *Forward Day by Day* writer today reminds us of this quote from John Muir, one of our country's most famous naturalists and conservationists. Muir was instrumental in forming the National Park Service and the Sierra Club. In spiritual direction, when I ask someone, "Where do you find meaning or feel closest to God?" the most frequent answer is "outdoors in nature."

In photosynthesis, trees transform light energy into chemical energy. I believe that the trees, the sun, the sky, the ocean, and the mountains also transform some energy inside of us when we are outdoors among them. We see beauty alive and well when before we could see only ugliness. We realize that there is something greater than ourselves, something that transcends our own problems. It is there for us. We do not have to pay for it. It is a gift.

My experience is that when I have difficulty sleeping because of physical, mental, or spiritual pain, it helps to go outside or sit by a window and watch the sunrise in the morning, even on a cloudy day. The sunrise, the world outside, can be a constant reminder of a new opening, a new beginning—the dawning of a fresh way to look at things.

Muir stands out as someone poised to make us aware of the marvel of nature, particularly the wilderness; but he also reminds us of our stewardship of this gift.

Consider the experience of viewing nature, the outdoors, as one of our most important lifesaving, life-renewing spiritual practices and remedies—better than drugs. But nature, like our own soul, also needs care and love.

Gerald May: Spiritual Direction

"Besides differing from psychotherapy in intent, content, and basic attitude, spiritual direction is generally surrounded by a characteristic atmosphere that is seldom encountered in any other interpersonal relationship…As one person put it, 'Being in spiritual direction is just like being in prayer, only there's someone with me in it.'"
—Gerald G. May in *Care of Mind/Care of Spirit: A Psychiatrist Explores Spiritual Direction* (HarperSanFrancisco, 1982), p. 113.

When I took down Dr. May's book *Care of Mind/Care of Spirit* from my bookshelf and opened it, a bulletin from September 1990 fell out. It mentioned a book group at my church that had been reading *Care of Mind/Care of Spirit*. There were no marks in the book, so I knew I had not read it. This happened over thirty years ago, two months before I went into recovery.

In the previous year, our book group had read May's book *Addiction and Grace*. For some reason, at that time I was not ready to hear May's words; but on this day it was different. In 1990, I was becoming a missionary member from my church, going out to start another Episcopal church in a growing part of our city. Alas, May's book would have been helpful in starting a new congregation as I began a life in recovery, and even more so nine years later when I was studying to become a deacon.

This has been one of the best books I have read about spiritual direction. Dr. May emphasizes how spiritual direction differs from his own highly effective psychotherapy. In therapy, the director or caregiver "hopes to encourage more efficient living in the prevailing culture, seeking to bolster an individual's capacity to achieve a sense of autonomous mastery over self and circumstances." Spiritual direction "seeks liberation from attachments and a self-giving surrender to the will of God."

This means that at some point spiritual direction may stand in opposition to many of the cultural standards and values supported by psychotherapy. May skillfully writes about how a spiritual director is constantly seeking out rabbit holes or traps the directee encounters while at the same time looking for God in his or her life. May also reminds us that the real healer is God, and that the director and directee are merely channels.

May cautions spiritual directors about how easy it is to become distorted in our roles, "playing God." This is a book I keep as close to me as possible while doing direction. I sometimes have to avoid obsessing about what *May would say* about something that comes up in a meeting. Then, after the time together, I hurry to look up the appropriate chapter. But, of course, May would say that our job is not to worry at that moment about what *we* say, but to concentrate solely and "most soulfully" on connecting this person to God during that moment!

Gerald May: God's Job

"In spiritual direction, one might say, 'My prayers are for God's will to be done in you and for your constant deepening in God. During this time that we are together I give myself, my awareness and attention and hopes and heart to God for you. I surrender myself to God for your sake.'"—Gerald May in *Care of Mind/Care of Spirit* (HarperSanFrancisco, 1982), p. 121.

In *Care of Mind/Care of Spirit*, May encourages us to begin our meeting for spiritual direction with a similar silent prayer—remembering that it is like being in prayer, except that we are with someone else and with God. We are to help direct the visitor or guest's attention, moment by moment, to God, at the same time knowing we can do this only if we are tuned in to our own prayer life.

May gives advice about how to bring up sexuality early in the sessions so it is an acceptable topic: "What are times you have felt closest to God? What about nature, music, sex, worship, or times of crisis?" May also makes a strong case for spiritual directors to be careful about relationships with their directees outside of the direction relationship. Dr. May's detailed chapter on referral is easily understood, especially because he writes about so many of his own personal experiences. Perhaps of greatest importance to those of us in the healing community is May's concept of the *difference between healing in the largest sense* and *curing a specific disorder*.

I am grateful that I have been in a group of spiritual directors that took May's advice and meet regularly to discuss concerns and issues that arise in our work. We meet for mutual support, prayer, and questioning, knowing that we are not doing this ministry alone, but are in community.

May asks us to identify in directees their experience of God beyond their belief system, emphasizing that belief and experience are two different areas to explore. It is important that we use the language of the directees' *own* spiritual experience and not our own. We should try to avoid solving people's spiritual problems with statements such as, "You should pray this way" or "You need to have more faith." May writes that the directee needs to know that the *desire* for an experience of God is *already* the experience of God that he or she is seeking.

I hope to remember that I am a companion, at most a midwife, on a person's heart-journey with God, and that this is *God's* business. God is in charge, even though I may *have such wonderful ideas!*

Gerald May: Spiritual Friends

"At the deepest level of our hearts we are all aching, for each other and for the same eternally loving One who calls us. It would be well, I think, if we could acknowledge this more often to one another."
—Gerald G. May in *Will and Spirit* (HarperOne, 1982), p. 321.

Gerald May in *Will and Spirit* writes that regardless of our tradition, the spiritual journey should not be undertaken alone. May quotes Kenneth Leech, who opens his book about spiritual direction, *Soul Friend* (Harper & Row, 1980), with the Celtic saying: "Anyone without a soul friend is a body without a head." A spiritual friend or guide is not one who *gives* directions, but one who *points* directions—a person who knows something of the terrain from having traveled some of it. Such a guide can say, "I think there may be trouble over there; perhaps try this way."

Professional training or qualifications of a director, counselor, or friend are not nearly as important as fundamental qualities of basic positive intent; humility (not presuming to know more than one knows); and willingness (commitment to traveling a rough road and allowing the guidance to come from God rather than trying to engineer it); and responding simply and directly to the needs of others as they are presented.

May cautions us that if we expect to be spiritual friends by learning techniques of discernment and using them on other people, the outcome will be nothing but a blind sales pitch or slightly pastoralized psychotherapy. He describes psychology as seeking to help a person solve the problems of living; while spiritual direction deepens the Question of life itself.

Gerald May: Love

"In speaking of love, narcissism says, 'I need you to love me.' Erotic love says, 'I need you.' Filial love says, 'I love you because I understand you.' Agape—if it could speak—might say, 'I *am* you *in* Love.'"
—Gerald G. May in *Will and Spirit* (HarperOne, 1982), p. 167.

In *Will and Spirit,* Gerald May discusses types of love: narcissistic (self-love), Me-Me; erotic (romantic) love, Me-You; filial (compassionate) love, I-Thou; and agape (divine, unconditional) love. May believes that erotic and filial love can act as "primary education leading to agape love." Our confusion comes when we expect unconditional love from human beings and expect conditional love from God—and look for unconditional love from an *image* of God.

May points out that those who believe they are as holy as God commit perhaps the greatest sin. Willful self-determination is a template for human evil, just as is willful vengeance. Willfulness always leads to separateness.

If we can move toward forgiveness for some past wrong, then our basic capacity for loving will not be injured. But if we hold on to resentment, it will become increasingly difficult to love or feel lovable. Our sense of separateness increases, and we become more and more afraid of anything resembling belonging, surrender, or union.

It is not so much the nature of evil forces that we experience, but *our response to them* that can make the difference in our lives. When faced with a difficult situation, we must not deaden ourselves to the reality, cop out, or react quickly with our own plan while forgetting to call on the active power of God. We are called to remember the importance of the situation and the need for action, but to factor in our total dependence on the unconditional love of God. Then our hearts can be open to God working in us—and at some deep level of our awareness, we can relax and be at peace.

Gerald May: Willingness and Surrender

"The gentlest form of spiritual narcissism is the idea that one can accomplish one's own spiritual growth. 'I can do it'."
—Gerald G. May in *Will and Spirit* (HarperOne, 1982), p. 115.

In *Will and Spirit,* Gerald May writes about struggles in our world today as well as our many battles within ourselves. We are likely to have issues with will, willingness, control, and surrender in our spiritual lives. Whenever we start our spiritual journey with *willingness,* as soon as we are aware of some spiritual growth, we become vulnerable to spiritual narcissism: the unconscious use of spiritual practices to increase our self-importance. We *try* to become holy, under the assumption that we can accomplish our own spiritual growth. This becomes *willfulness* masquerading as *willingness.*

When we gain an awareness of our own self-interest as to why we are participating in charitable works, these actions and gifts will be better given and received. Sin occurs when self-image and personal willfulness become so important that one forgets, represses, or denies one's absolute connectedness and grounding in *the God within us,* the power who creates and sustains the cosmos and who placed in us that yearning.

May encourages us to allow attachments to come or go rather than constantly clinging to them. We must be aware of our need for self-importance; and thus he cautions us about immediately leaping to shore ourselves up. He places less emphasis on coping and mastery, and more on *waking up to whatever is happening in the present moment.*

As we surrender some of our self-importance, we make friends with mystery. Even though we may not necessarily always find God when we sacrifice our self-importance, May believes that as we lose our *need* for self-importance, we realize that *God has already found us.* We will experience more spontaneity and awareness when we are not driven to perform and can let things *flow:* when we no longer need to be defined through self-judgment or evaluation of our own actions.

May reminds us that spirituality cannot be a means to end our discomfort.

Spiritual growth has to be a way into life, not an escape from it. We are called to be *in* the world, not *of* the world—and unfortunately this *of the world* side may be uncomfortable.

If you are familiar with the statue of the Return of the Prodigal Son in the Bishop's Garden at the National Cathedral, this is an icon for surrender and willingness.

Bourgeault: The Lens Through Which You see

"If you wear glasses, you likely often forget that they're even there! Only when you take the lenses off do you realize how much your capacity to see is informed by the lens through which you are seeing, or as Richard Rohr often says, *'How* we see is *what* we see.'"

—Cynthia Bourgeault in *The Shape of God: Deepening the Mystery of the Trinity* (CAC, 2004), disc 2.

Here Cynthia is using an analogy to teach us about the Trinity; but we can apply this also to our everyday life. If you or the person you are meeting with for spiritual direction wears glasses, try this exercise:

Take off your glasses. Try to see at a distance or read a passage of text. Perhaps you will "see" or realize that what you "see" actually depends on the lenses of your glasses. Often our lens, or how we see the world, is through the filter of our work, our family, or our position. We might experience a need for prestige; a desire for money or control or power; a longing to be in the spotlight, or successful; or we could be obsessed with beauty, clothes, food, alcohol, drugs, or controlled by other addictions. When our world or the sun is too bright, we need to put on sunglasses. At other times, if we are depressed or grieving, we truly may see the world through *dark* glasses.

Meditate, pray about, and write a description of the lenses *you* use to view your family, friends, enemies, the world. In our attempt to stay connected to God individually and in community, we hope we will connect to the Christ in ourselves and the Christ in our neighbor. Let us learn to see ourselves and the world and others through the lens of the fruit of the spirit: love, joy, peace, forbearance (patience), kindness, goodness, faithfulness, gentleness, and self-control (Galatians 5:22-23).

Some say spiritual direction is helping someone become awake. Spiritual direction can help us put on a new pair of glasses.

The Liesborn Prayer Wheel

"Sometimes returning to ancient sources is exactly what we need to renew our spiritual lives."
—Payton Dodd, Jana Riess, and David Van Biema in "Foreword," *The Prayer Wheel: A Daily Guide to Renewing Your Faith with a Rediscovered Spiritual Practice* (Convergent, 2018).

Three well-known religion writers join forces to present a meditative method using the ancient practice of the prayer wheel. The medieval Liesborn Wheel consists of four concentric bands containing the Lord's Prayer; the Old Testament Gifts of the Spirit from Isaiah; Events in the Life of Jesus; and the Beatitudes. Each of these four texts is divided into seven stepping-stones. Together these texts comprise a complete vocabulary of faith.

The seven phrases or petitions or stepping-stones are spiritual tools or disciplines to put us in position to connect to the God within us. The authors suggest journeying around the wheel as a daily prayer practice. The wheel can also be used topically for special needs, in times of grief, when offering gratitude, or when praying for others. Its use is appropriate in times of joy, discernment, or needing forgiveness. The wheel can aid prayers for healing, hope, praise, and achieving calmness. It also can be a guide for Bible study. There are endless possibilities.

The invitation to return to this ancient source is an opportunity for all of us who would like to learn alternative ways to experience contemplative prayer.

Movie Date

"I have a theory that movies operate on the level of dreams, where you dream yourself."
—Meryl Streep.

My granddaughter, Zoe, and I have been having a date for many years on Friday afternoon to watch old movies. I wish we could swim together or stroll in the woods or walk down some of Little Rock's beautiful trails; but my physical disability makes that too difficult. However, we can curl up in the king-size bed in our master bedroom, all lights out, each covered by our favorite blankets, while we eat popcorn and watch movies. We have seen almost every musical made. Occasionally we watch drama, and less often, comedy. This week Zoe saw, for the first time, *Some Like It Hot*. I forgot to mention that Zoe is going into the tenth grade, and usually I get permission from her parents for her to see certain movies. We usually talk a little about the movie after it is over. Sometimes there is much to talk about; at other times, very little.

In the past I have shown her paintings from my favorite art museums, and rarely have we read poetry together. There is so much grandparents want to share with their precious grandchildren. Mostly, however, it is just about the pleasure of being in their presence. I have learned to drop everything I am doing and be with her if she sends a text about a potential movie date.

This movie date has become for me an icon of what prayer time may be about. I think there is some built-in homing device through which both we and God yearn for each other's presence.

Prayer is occasionally words, but mostly presence. I think God longs to share God's experience, God's amazing world with us; but mostly God longs for *our* presence—just as there is a conscious, and maybe even a stronger *unconscious* longing in us just to be in God's presence.

Gould: Kindness

"Good and kind people outnumber all others by thousands to one. The tragedy of human history lies in the enormous potential for destruction in rare acts of evil, not in the high frequency of evil people. Complex systems can only be built step by step, whereas destruction requires but an instant. Thus, in what I like to call the Great Asymmetry, every spectacular incident of evil will be balanced by 10,000 acts of kindness, too often unnoticed and invisible as the 'ordinary' efforts of a vast majority."
—Stephen Jay Gould in *The New York Times* (9/26/2001).

A longtime friend, Dr. Steve Thomason, Dean of St. Mark's Cathedral, Seattle, sent out this nearly twenty-year-old Gould quote several months ago for all of us to consider. Humans seem unable to avoid being dualistic, viewing life as a well-balanced struggle between good and evil. In fact, it is difficult to avoid considering evil and failure and missing the mark to have the greater power and strength over us in our lives. We receive all "A"s but one "B" on our report card. We agonize and only remember the "B." We remember only the one line we missed in our class play and discount the brilliant lines we remembered. We obsess over our rejection letters rather than celebrating our college acceptance or recent job promotion. We physicians think daily about the diagnosis we missed and forget about the thousands we correctly made. We forgot to visit our friend the week or day before she dies, but in our grief we discount all the hundreds of other visits we made during her illness.

The morning, noon, evening, and late night news can seem overwhelming when we are told about all the human tragedies, deaths, and violence. On a good day, perhaps there is one last thirty-second segment about someone's kindness.

Gould, evolutionary biologist and historian of science, contends that the forces in the world are not evenly divided, and that reality is overwhelmingly composed of kindness, not evil. Gould believes the problem is that these acts of kindness are so small that they go unnoticed. Evil and failure stops us in our tracks, immediately gets our attention, and blinds us with its bright orange blare.

How can we put on a fresh pair of glasses and begin to see the world differently? That is the pathway to even more obvious acts of kindness. It begins with a small, simple step called *gratitude*. I have so many friends who survive unbelievable tragedy by making and reciting a gratitude list each day, most often at night before they go to sleep. I have spiritual friends who even send me their daily gratitude list. By their act, they are encouraging me to do the same.

Gould is challenging us to remember the kind acts we see constantly, especially when we feel overcome by some act of evil and begin to believe that darkness has overtaken our world.

Gibran: On Children, Steady Bow, Smorgasbord

"Your children are not your children.

You may give them your love but not your thoughts,

For they have their own thoughts.

You are the bows from which your children

as living arrows are sent forth.

The archer sees the mark upon the path of the infinite,

and He bends you with His might

that His arrows may go swift and far.

Let your bending in the archer's hand be for gladness;

For even as he loves the arrow that flies,

so He loves also the bow that that is stable."

—Khalil Gibran, "On Children" in *The Prophet* (1923).

This may be some of the best advice about relating to our children we can find. Parents are to be the steady or stable "bow." Our children do not belong to us. They are the most important guests we will ever have in our home.

Another piece of wisdom came to us from a counselor, Phyllis Raney, who led a parenting class at our church. She told us our job was to provide the best smorgasbord of possibilities of experiences for our children to sample. What they choose, however, is up to them. We are to be the best possible providers of opportunities for them to experience; but we cannot control their decision as to what they become interested in.

We have three children, and as parents we had busy lives as physicians at a children's hospital. We wondered how to give quality individual time to each of our children. At the birth of our second child, my mother-in-law gave me a book, *Promises to Peter* (Word Books, 1974), by Charlie Shedd. We read in it about taking each child out to dinner one night a week. We let the child choose the restaurant, within reason. So, one night a week, usually Monday, was "date night" with one of our children. It was a gift to concentrate on letting that child tell his or her story without distractions, and to appreciate how much you loved him or her.

We also went to many medical meetings each year and tried to take one child with us, again hoping to spend quality time one on one. This was one more offering on the smorgasbord.

Our children are older now, with children of their own. It is easier to be the steady bow.

The steady bow image has now also become an image for our relationship for God. We learned about it as we tried to raise our children. Now it is teaching us more about how God cares for us. The smorgasbord has also become the image of the innumerable ways God has provided for us to learn more about this one who so loves us like a parent.

Death and Relationships

"We are given each other in trust. I think people are much too wonderful to be alive briefly and gone." —Marilynne Robinson.

When I talk with spiritual friends who have experienced the death of a loved one, I remind them that the God of my understanding does not give us an amazingly loving relationship with someone else and then abruptly take it away. Death is not a period at the end of a sentence but more like a comma. The relationship still goes on.

Our loved ones continue in relationship with us, but in a way that we don't yet understand. We can sometimes feel their presence. We often intuit the reality of their prayers. Frederick Buechner has written in his book, *A Crazy, Holy Grace* (Zondervan, 2017), about doing active imagination with those we still love who have died. We can converse with them in the silence of our mind; but often we merely *feel* their presence, supporting and loving us just as they did when they were alive.

I also remind friends that those we love are now with us at all times—beside us—again, in some form we do not understand. When they were alive, we were present with them only when we saw them physically. They are now always with us in a closer relationship than we can explain.

Love Never Dies

"Love never dies."—1 Corinthians 13:8.

I have heard this passage from 1 Corinthians about love so many times; but when I heard it this Sunday, directly from our friend Paul and our preacher Michael McCain, I was moved to tears. I have told people who are grieving that the love they have for and from their loved one is still there and never dies.

I don't understand it. It is a mystery. I know I look at pictures of my loved ones who have died, my brother and my grandparents, and I can feel their love as I send my love to them. Frederick Buechner and Henri Nouwen tell us that our bodies die, but our mutual love somehow returns to God and is kept for all eternity. If you are a mystic, you have no difficulty understanding this. If you are a person who comprehends mainly by rational thinking, this may be a difficult concept.

Why did this passage so move me on Sunday? As I grow older, I have been obsessing about how I will miss friends and family members when we become separated by death. Suddenly I know in my heart that the love we have for each other will always endure. Our love for them is ongoing, as is their love for us. We will never be lonely. I believe that in some mysterious way this love never dies and is carried forward to be a transforming effect in ourselves and in the universe.

Love Never Dies Again

"But soon we shall die and all memory of those five will have left the earth, and we ourselves shall be loved for a while and forgotten. But the love will have been enough; all those impulses of love return to the love that made them. Even memory is not necessary for love. There is a land of the living and a land of the dead and the bridge is love, the only survival, the only meaning."—Thornton Wilder in *The Bridge of San Luis Rey* (HarperCollins, 1927), p. 107.

In his Foreword to *The Bridge of San Luis Rey*, Russell Banks reminds us that at the memorial service in New York for British victims of the attack on the World Trade Center, British Prime Minister Tony Blair read these closing sentences of Thornton Wilder's novel. We hope that those we love will know our love throughout all eternity. We also want to tell them about those we have loved, such as our parents and siblings and the grandparents that they may not have known.

I think Paul in his first letter to the Corinthians and Wilder in this novel are both telling us that *the best of this love we have for each other never ever dies*. This is a mystery, but I know in my heart it is true.

This February 12th would have been my mother's ninety-seventh birthday. We did not always appreciate each other; but today I feel her love. My parents died before I was ordained a deacon and before the birth of any of our grandchildren. Though my parents are not physically here, their love still surrounds us. All of the people in the picture at my parents' wedding are now dead; but I so often feel lifted up by their presence in prayer and love. There are days when I feel a love whose only source may be *the God of love;* but at other times I sense a love from specific individuals who have died.

I think of the group of women with whom I have been reading books once a week for more years than I can count. After a recommendation from one of our members, Lisa Brandom, we undertook reading Wilder's *The Bridge of San Luis Rey* as our recent literary journey. I feel the love of each of these women every time we meet. One friend reminds us that she would keep coming, even if we were only reading the phone book.

I now know that I will feel their love in my heart for years to come, even after we are no longer able to meet. Love is all we have to contribute to this life that will be lasting. Love is all we will carry with us into the life of the resurrection. Love is the bridge between these two territories.

Hours and Angels

"We are always meeting *dead*lines; we are always running out of time. The message of *following* the *monastic* hours is to live daily with the real rhythms of the day. We learn to listen to the music of this moment. We learn to dance a little in our hearts, to open our inner gates a crack more, to hearken to the music of silence, the divine life breath of the universe."—David Steindl-Rast, O.S.B., in *The Music of Silence: Entering the Sacred Space of Monastic Experience* (HarperCollins, 1995).

I take this book off my shelf to see two cards drop out, both from deceased spiritual friends. The one from Nyna Keeton is an encouraging note about some of my writing. Another from Joanne Meadors is on a card from San Marco Museum in Florence, Italy, depicting the Fra Angelico painting of the angel beating the drum from *The Tabernacle of the Linaioli*. The angels playing the harp and the trumpet are also on a card from another spiritual friend with whom I have lost contact.

There is also a photograph of the musical Fra Angelico angels on the altarpiece at the Pierce Chapel at Trinity Cathedral, Little Rock. I remember I went on a trip to Florence solely to see these angels. A book full of angels, a book full of memories still being communicated from spiritual friends I no longer physically see— calling me back to the spiritual life we shared.

Also, between the pages of the book is a *Forward Day by Day* pamphlet about following the monastic hours. This was my first introduction to the hours over thirty years ago. Years later I would read so many of Phyllis Tickle's writings about her experience with the monastic hours. *The Music of Silence* is also an invitation to journey through the day by keeping the monastic hours in some manner. Each of the eight hours is prayerfully described by Brother David, often using the images of the Fra Angelico angels.

Beware of cards and notes you leave in books for unknown reasons. They may become messages from angels unaware.

Buechner: Memory, Eucharist, Jesus

"There are two ways of remembering. One way is to make an excursion from the living present back into the dead past. The other way is to summon the dead past back into the living present. The young widow remembers her husband, and he is there beside her. When Jesus said, 'Do this in remembrance of me,' he was not prescribing a periodic slug of nostalgia."—Frederick Buechner in *Wishful Thinking* (Harper & Row, 1973).

Buechner gives us two ways to remember, going back and bringing memories forward. Going back to past memories can allow us to relive a scene from our lives. Anthony de Mello writes that perhaps that scene was too powerful to experience the first time. As we relive it, we can take part in it again and again, each time gaining a greater sense of its meaning.

Bringing memories forward is like doing active imagination with a living friend or with someone you deeply loved who has died. You imagine the person's presence with you. My experience is that sometimes you feel that presence even without trying to imagine it.

Buechner believes that when Jesus said, "Do this in remembrance of me" (1 Corinthians 11:24b), he was calling us to *bring him back* into our presence—to know and feel his love, so we might go out and bring others in to share in this love.

Some believe that Jesus is actually present in the bread and wine at the Eucharist. Others believe that the bread and wine are messengers or symbols, reminding us of Jesus' presence and love in our lives. Either way, the God of love is present.

Rohr: Forgiveness

"As long as you can deal with evil by some means other than forgiveness, you will keep projecting, fearing, and attacking it over there, instead of 'gazing' on it within and 'weeping' over it within yourself and all of us. Forgiveness demands three new simultaneous 'seeings': I must see God in the other; I must access God in myself; and I must experience God in a new way that is larger than an 'Enforcer.'" —Adapted from Richard Rohr's *Things Hidden: Scripture as Spirituality* (Franciscan Media, 2008), pp. 193-194.

Richard Rohr is teaching us more basic lessons about how to forgive. It involves seeing the Christ—God in the person we are forgiving—as well as seeing God or Christ in ourselves. That makes sense. But then Rohr throws in this third condition. We see that God is more, larger than a hall monitor handing out detention slips, checking a list, looking at our every action and judging whether we and our neighbors are behaving rightly.

My experience is that we are called to enlarge our concept of God as a God of love. How do we do this? We place ourselves with other people who seem to experience God's love. We observe the ways in which they know how to forgive others.

As we see the Christ in others who know love, the God of love, the Christ in us awakens—and slowly, often *very* slowly, we begin to see the Christ also in those who have harmed us. We may discover that personal tragedies have brought them to the place of hurting others. This awareness starts to come as we pray daily, sometimes hourly, for the person who has harmed us. We realize we are still carrying around a heavy load of resentment that is like a cancer, destroying the joy in our lives a little each day. That person is still hurting us. He or she is becoming our higher power, our God, because more and more, that is all we can think about.

As we daily pray for that person, he or she may never change; but my experience is that *we will.*

Vamping

"Music is the language of the spirit. It opens the secret of life, bringing peace, abolishing strife." —Kahlil Gibran.

Once a week I play harp duets with a very talented harpist who tolerates my missed or absent notes and tries to teach an old harpist new tricks and fingering. Today Pam also taught me an unfamiliar word, *vamping*. She said, "I will vamp you in." She plays a brief series of chords before I start my part of the piece. I definitely like the word. Vamping. It means we play a simple chord or beat, usually as we wait for someone else to start—and then perhaps keep quietly playing the background chords as the other player takes the melody.

I think this best describes what meeting with a spiritual friend is like. I may ask a simple question, such as, "Where did you see God in your life today?" I may then repeat the question when the subject seems to change. Often I keep saying prayers that the Holy Spirit will guide us. These prayers are my chords.

Our job is to stay connected to the beat, as we listen for the rhythm and melody of the presence of the Holy Spirit. We are to stay in the background and support and undergird the person we are with. We keep the beat going and listen and pray so the Holy Spirit can come in strong, guiding and directing us both.

May: Other Religious Traditions, Connections

"We are all rooted together in the ground of consciousness that is God's gift to all of us, and our joining is absolute. When the Islamic mullah prays with true and quiet heart, I believe that the souls of the Iowa farmer and the Welsh miner are touched. When the gong sounds in the Japanese monastery and the monks enter the timeless silence of Zazen, their quiet nourishes the Brazilian native and the Manhattan executive. When Jews and Christians pray with true willingness, the Hindu scientist and the Russian policeman are enriched."

—Gerald G. May in *Will and Spirit* (HarperOne, 1982), pp. 319–320.

Many authors remind us of our connection to Nature and to the world around us. Others remind us of our connection to the poor, the weak, the sick, the lonely. Gerald May reminds us of our connection to other religions—how the Spirit moves in so many different paths that we do not understand Too deep for words.

There is more here, though, than just recognizing God at work in so many varied ways. May is also telling us *we are intimately connected by this Spirit*. What we do to further the Spirit, to connect to God in our own day, in our own way, makes a difference across the globe in some distant rain forest.

Again, this relationship is a deep mystery beyond our knowing. Sometimes when I read this passage from May, I can sit and almost feel the Iowa farmer working his black dirt, since we spent four years in Iowa City in training. Then I try to cross the Atlantic to England. I can connect to the shepherd and his dogs and sheep striding through green pastures, since we have made several trips to England and Scotland.

Because of our political situation these days, I am having more difficulty connecting to the people in Russia. I have never been there; but I always wanted to go to St. Petersburg to see Rembrandt's *Return of the Prodigal Son* in the Hermitage Museum. The next time I watch a newscast from Russia, I will look and try to imagine the people there. I think this could make a difference. I hope they are doing the same for us.

Spiritual Compass

"Within each one of us there is a spiritual compass. It points always toward the good, toward what is holy. The compass is made of our values, what we believe and hold sacred, and over the years our experience makes the compass within us even more accurate, refining our ability to seek the right direction in life, making us even more sensitive to the pull of compassion and common sense. Therefore, we do not have to be afraid that we will get lost, wandering the wilderness of this age. We only have to follow where our heart leads and our reason points the way."—Bishop Steven Charleston Daily Facebook Page.

Cynthia Bourgeault would agree with Steven Charleston about a spiritual compass. She calls it an inward GPS (Global Positioning System), similar to the one we use in our car to get us to the right location. What we need to know is *where we are*—and then the address of where we *want to go*—and the GPS will get us there.

Sometimes we are uncertain *where* we are; but we have a good idea of where we *want* to go. Our aim above all is to keep our connection to God. I love it when our ideal location is not yet on the map, and the GPS takes us as close as possible. This also may be true in regard to our spiritual life.

Bourgeault calls our heart a "God Positioning System." When it is attuned, turned on, it will allow us to achieve balance in a whole different way: perceiving by separating and differentiating things from each other; perceiving the whole and discerning our place within the whole. For her, becoming attuned to this spiritual GPS comes through the contemplative practice of Centering Prayer.

 Cynthia Bourgeault, *The Shape of God: Deepening the Mystery of the Trinity* (CAC, 2004), disc 4.

Cynthia Bourgeault, "How Change Happens" in *Transgression* (CAC, 2014), Vol. 2 No. 1, p. 86.

Centering Prayer Guidelines

"1. Choose a sacred word as the symbol of your intention to consent to God's presence and action within.

2. Sitting comfortably and with eyes closed, settle briefly and silently introduce the sacred word as the symbol of your consent to God's presence and action within.

3. When engaged with your thoughts, feelings, images, and reflections, return ever-so-gently to the sacred word.

4. At the end of the prayer period (20 minutes), remain in silence with eyes closed for a couple of minutes."

—Contemplative Outreach, Ltd., contemplative outreach.org.

Reviewing and remembering the guidelines for Centering Prayer are worth repeating. This contemporary form of the ancient practice of contemplative or listening prayer has been described by Catholic monks Thomas Merton, Thomas Keating, and Basil Pennington, as well as Quaker Richard Foster. It is drawn from ancient prayer practices of the Desert Mothers and Fathers, *The Cloud of the Unknowing,* Teresa of Avila, and St. John of the Cross.

At a recent retreat at our church, Steve Standiford, a friend from New York City associated with Contemplative Outreach has practiced Centering Prayer for more than twenty years. He reminded us of how to deepen our relationship with God. He uses this familiar illustration to help us to experience God's presence and love in our lives through Centering Prayer: "A first-time tourist to New York

City gets into the cab and asks the driver, 'How do you get to Carnegie Hall?' The driver responds, 'Practice, practice, practice!'"

Thoreau: Superficial Life

"When our life ceases to be inward and private, conversation degenerates into mere gossip. We rarely meet a man who can tell us any news which he has not read in a newspaper, or been told by his neighbor. …In proportion as our inward life fails, we go more constantly and desperately to the post office. You may depend on it, that the poor fellow who walks away with the greatest number of letters proud of his extensive correspondence has not heard from himself this long while."—Henry David Thoreau.

My spiritual director sent this to me today. Most of us do not go to the post office, and letter writing is becoming a lost art. But we are now judged by how many Facebook friends we have! I have a Facebook page to keep informed about family and friends. But a Facebook message is very different from a phone call or a visit or a conversation over a meal. When we are face to face, we can share what is really going on with us. It is then that we may bare our soul and look for the Christ in our friend—and hope that the Christ within us will guide us. Meeting with spiritual friends is not optional for the inner life, the life of the soul. It is mandatory.

Even better is meeting over a meal. Replenishing our bodies mysteriously opens up our mind to nourish the soul. Here is where we see Christ in each other, and maybe even get a brief glimpse of the Christ in ourselves.

I have previously told you about a pediatric radiology medical group I was a part of for over than thirty years. We each had our own agenda and our areas of expertise. We were having difficulty making decisions and seeing the importance of each other's plans. We decided to meet for lunch once a week and just talk to each other about what was going on in our lives. It took a while, but miracles happened. We began to look at each other's ideas in a better light. The mysterious result of meeting and talking to each other and having a regularly shared meal was that the food and conversation nourished us into forming a genuine community.

Live Your Life, Gratitude

"Live your life so that the fear of death can never enter your heart. When you arise in the morning, give thanks for the morning light. Give thanks for your life and strength. Give thanks for your food and for the joy of living. And if perchance you see no reason for giving thanks, rest assured the fault is in yourself."—Ascribed to Chief Tecumseh.

Gratitude is definitely a secret to a Spirit-filled life. Those in 12-step recovery groups believe that we are less likely to go back to our old addiction—what they call "a slip"—if we continue in the way of gratitude each day. Whenever someone in recovery is not doing well, the most-suggested remedy is to make a gratitude list to refer to daily, especially at night.

The insight from Trees for Life founder Balbir Mathur that he "travels in a boat called Surrender. His two oars are Forgiveness and Gratitude" which serve as a guide for our life. As long as we can surrender to a power greater than ourselves and are willing to forgive and remain grateful for what we have been given, we live a life of peace. Our blood pressure stays closer to normal. We are less likely to become irritated at all of life's hiccups: our computer is not responding; someone has said something unkind; We have expectations of ourselves and others that are not being met; our body is not working the way it should; We are not getting our way or achieving our plan for the day.

Guided by forgiveness and gratitude, we can live assured that there is a grand plan beyond our own.

My husband and I once made fun of an older man, a friend of his father's, who so often said, "You must have an attitude of gratitude." Well, we both know now that there is no greater wisdom for living than this simple formula.

Marrying Orthodoxy to Orthopraxis

"There's a movement in the church to marry action and contemplation, to connect orthodoxy and orthopraxis. We're not throwing out the things we believe, but we're also focusing on practices that work out those beliefs. In the past few decades Christianity has primarily been about what we believe. But in Jesus we see an invitation to join our actions with a movement rather than ideas and doctrine. People have grown tired of a Christianity that can say what it believes on paper but doesn't have anything to show with our lives."—Adapted from Shane Claiborne, *When Action Meets Contemplation* (Center for Action and Contemplation, 2010), disc 1.

Orthopraxis, or practicing our faith, differs from orthodoxy, an adherence to a certain belief. It is a paradox. We need both. We need to frame and reframe what we believe; but if we do not put that belief into practice, we are like a "noisy gong." I am one of those people Shane Claiborne talks about who has lots of t-shirts spelling out social justice issues—but until I write letters or make phone calls or visit those in prisons or those who are sick or in trouble,

I am not putting that belief into practice. I have learned this most pointedly from younger people. The women in my family marched in the women's march the day after the recent presidential inauguration. We were talking with our feet. We were inspired to do more by the crowds and speakers at this protest.

That day has become like an icon for me about reaching out from the words of my comfortable t-shirt and visiting and making calls and protecting those in need. I know in my heart that this is the way the Spirit works. We are called to study about God and the Spirit, but we are also compelled to find the God *within ourselves* that will lead us to discover the God in others.

I share with spiritual friends that when I am attempting to find God in others, God is most apparent in those in need. God most readily shines in those who are sick or dying or seeking recovery, or in those at our food pantry or at our dinners for homeless veterans. Practicing the ministry of orthopraxy teaches us the most about orthodoxy, about God.

Nouwen, Lawrence: Unceasing Praying, *Fiddler*

"Our minds are always active. Do we have to become victims of our unceasing thought? No, we can convert our unceasing thinking into unceasing prayer by making our inner monologue into a continuing dialogue with our God, who is the source of all love."—Henri Nouwen in *Bread for the Journey* (HarperSanFrancisco, 1997).

The book to turn to first, to understand unceasing prayer, is *Practicing the Presence of God*. It is a very small collection of the teachings and experiences of Brother Lawrence, a French Carmelite monk who was the cook for his community in Paris in the 17th century. Father Joseph Beaufort compiled he book from letters and four conversations with Brother Lawrence, as he described his walk with God—not from the head, but within his heart. He saw God in every aspect, in every second of his life as he washed pots and pans, purchased wine, or cooked the meals—continually conversing with God. He never became weary of doing insignificant things for the love of God—believing that intervals of prayer should not differ from other times; seeing God as a friend he would not want to be estranged from; feeling God's presence more acutely in sickness than in good health.

My favorite fictional role model for continually being in conversation with God is Tevye in the 1971 American dramatic musical, *Fiddler on the Roof.*

I try to watch the movie several times a year and go to see the play whenever it comes close to Little Rock. It is long but so worth

163

journeying with Tevye in his persistent conversations with God through many trials.

I Look for God When I Do the Dishes

"I search for the Spirit as I take out the trash. The sacred is revealed in brilliant light only rarely, in the flash of some great insight unexpected, but much more than this the holy is to be discovered in our daily lives, in the moments when we are simply being ourselves. Putting the kids to bed, working in the garden, sitting on the porch in the evening: the beauty of eternity is that it hides in plain sight all around us. We are all prophets of the predictable pattern, witnesses to the wonder of the average day." —Bishop Steven Charleston Daily Facebook Page.

The God of my understanding uses every bit of our lives to call us to God's love. I remember one morning walk around my block when I took notice of all the trash bins out in front of houses. I suddenly realized on this walk that many of the spiritual disciplines we practice are simply to clear our minds—literally taking out the trash so we can hear God speak to our lives.

Bishop Charleston is reminding us of Brother Lawrence's experience in *Practicing the Presence of God,* seeking and seeing God in every aspect of our life. He is telling us we don't have to live in a monastery to find and live this kind of life. He believes we can know God's presence more in our daily routine rather than in some St. Paul-like, blinding, falling-off-our-horse, spectacular event.

Bishop Charleston is also practicing the family systems axiom of trying to live a less anxious presence in the world around him. He is looking around with awe at the ever-changing beauty of God's immanence in the vastness of nature and being transformed by what he sees. He is actively seeking Christ in every place and every person he encounters. This is the spiritual discipline of living in the present moment.

What I Learned at VBS

"Help me slow down, Jesus.

Hheellpp mmee ssllooww ddoowwnn JJEEUUSS.

Hhheeelllppp   mmmeee   ssslllooowww   dddoowwwnnn, JJJEEEUUUSSS.

Hhhheeeelllllpppp,   mmmmeeee,   ssssllllooooowwww ddddoooowwwwnnnn, JJJJEEEEUUUUSSSS."

—"Bible Story Teller" in *Rolling River Rampage: Experience the Ride of a Lifetime with God!* (Cokesbury VBS, 2018).

My friend, Mary Manning, and I were the storytellers at St. Mark's Vacation Bible School (VBS) last summer. I have been the storyteller at VBS at the other churches I served, but I always did it alone. It was so amazing to have a partner. Mary is a retired schoolteacher. I am a retired teacher of medical school students and residents and fellows; but Mary had a lot to teach me. I had decided how to tell the story for each group. At our first meeting, Mary suggested we do it another way. She was so right. I keep thinking what it would have been like if she had not been there with me. It could have been a disaster.

Now I know why Jesus sent the disciples out two by two. At my late stage of life, I am learning that almost any ministry is better with a partner, if possible. We learn so much from each other's experience and expertise.

This prayer for today about slowing down was our favorite one in connection with the story of Mary and Martha. I try to say it during my day, every day.

I learned one more thing at VBS. Mary and I were with each group of children for only twenty minutes. We told stories about Jesus calling the disciples; Mary and Martha; Zacchaeus; the Last Supper; and Jesus sending his disciples out with the assurance that he would be with them always. Each day before telling the new story, we would review the story from the previous day. I was amazed that the children in each group, even the four-year-olds, remembered so much of yesterday's story. Of course, each story was reinforced through crafts and music and games.

VBS taught me that what we teach and what we say can be like seeds planted to germinate in children's hearts at some later date. I am reminded of teachers I had at VBS who taught me about the love of God through stories. I want to be like them.

Nouwen: Reimaging and Reimagining

"When we believe that we are created in the image of God himself and come to realize that Christ came to let us reimagine this, then meditation and prayer can lead us to our true identity."—Henri Nouwen in *You Are the Beloved* (Convergent Books, 2017).

I have spent much of my professional life has imaging children with X-rays, ultrasound, nuclear imaging, CT, and MRI. I am intrigued by Nouwen's insight that the Incarnation is a reimaging of God. Reimaging in radiology usually means taking a second look. If we are uncertain of what we saw the first time, we take another picture. When we see something we cannot quite understand, we produce another image to see if it is still there. We want to verify that what we saw the first time was real—so we take another picture, sometimes at a different angle.

Reimagining, on the other hand, means to form a new concept. Jesus came to reimage God, to show us a God of love with skin on. He also came to help us reimagine God, to enable us to realize a new relationship with a loving God. The Incarnation is pivotal in bringing us new concepts of love in our relationship with each other and with God.

Reimage and reimagine that.

Nouwen: Beloved for All Eternity

"God loved you before you were born. God will love you after you die. God says, 'I have loved you with an everlasting love.' You belong to God from eternity to eternity. Life is just a little opportunity during a few years to say, 'I love you, too.'"—Henri Nouwen in *You Are the Beloved: Daily Meditations for Spiritual Living* (Convergent Books, 2017).

Nouwen is reminding us we were loved before we were born and will be loved after we die. Love never dies. We brought love into the world and we have the opportunity to enlarge and multiply it and give thanks for it. We also in some mysterious way leave part of love behind and take some part of love with us when we die.

Love is the inheritance, the legacy we leave behind in the world. Death has no power over love. If only we could keep remembering that our true vocation on this earth is *to love:* to let members of our family know they are loved; to let our neighbor know he or she is loved; to let those in our city, those in our state, those in our country, and those in our world know they are loved. This is a monumental job, but we will be given times and places every day to do this. It may not always be on our agenda, but if we are open to it, we will find opportunities to respond. David G. Benner, in *Spirituality and the Awakening Self: The Sacred Journey of Transformation* (Brazos Press, 2012), calls this awareness *enlightenment*—seeing with the eyes of the heart (pp. 144-146). He also believes this is a gift of the Spirit that is readily available.

Lewis Hines

"He arrived at the coal mines, textile mills and industrial factories dressed in a three-piece suit. He was just a humble Bible salesman, he claimed, who wanted to spread the good word to the laborers inside. What Lewis Hines actually wanted was to take photos of those laborers—and show the world what it looked like when children were put to work."—Jessica Contrera, "The Searing Photos That Helped End Child Labor in America" in *The Washington Post* (9/3/2018).

This important article by Jessica Contrera in *The Washington Post* reminds us how art can change the world. Most of us know the story. Hines was a photographer in the early 1900s and who photographed the horrendous working conditions of young children laboring in mines, in factories, and in any business that employed unskilled workers.

Our hearts break when we see these young girls and boys just slightly older than toddlers working long shifts in dangerous conditions. Their faces are dull. There are few smiles. They were in essence slave labor.

I love seafood, but almost every time I eat oysters now I see a childish girl photographed by Hines of maybe six or seven, with her yellow hair pulled back, standing on a stool to reach the table to shuck oysters with the older women. If you have ever shucked oysters, you know it is a dirty task that sprays mud all over you and includes the hazard of cuts from a slip of the oyster knife. It is not an easy job for adults, much less for children.

Oyster shells form the floor of the bleak room. The young girl's apron is almost as big as she is. We do not see her face. That might be too much to bear. We do see the faces of the women—perhaps relatives—working beside her. They look older than their presumed ages, with hapless expressions on their faces.

Photographic exposure to such scenes mobilizes our country and leads to labor laws for children. Hines not only shares these dramatic pictures of children doing tasks dangerous even for adults, he reveals the children's ages and tells us their stories. Hines' story to accompany this image is of "seven-year-old Rosie. Regular shucker. Her second year at it. Illiterate. Works all day. Only shucks a few pots a day. Varn & Platt Canning Co., Bluffton, South Carolina, published February 1913" (*Library of Congress Photographs Online Catalog*).

Hines' work is a reminder that art, photography, music, writing, and stories are as powerful as guns and cannons to the revolutions of history. When I talk with people about how they want to change the world, I remind them of how this one person with one camera and maybe a Bible in hand made a difference.

We are not all Lewis Hines, but we have been created with talents that can make differences in others' lives just as he did—with no threat of violence.

We discover and activate the difference we can make by connecting to the Christ within us. We become the person God created us to be and discern and share each important gift.

God Callings

"The many things we have to do, the hundred and one calls on our time and attention, don't get between ourselves and God. On the contrary, they are to us in very truth his Body and his Blood."
—H. A. Williams in *The Joy of God* (Templegate, 1992).

Well, this is a novel idea! We anticipate during the day the quiet time that we will have writing or walking or practicing Centering Prayer; but the interactions we have with people during the day and at work are just as much a part of our relationship with God!

The God within us is meeting with the God in our neighbor or the patients we work with, or our coworkers or our partners, or the children we teach or our fellow students. This is like turning on a switch in our brain. Our life is not divided into parts. Every part of our being is an offering. Every second, every hour is an opportunity to share the love we have been so freely given. We should tape this Williams' quote to the back of our cell phones to read whenever we get that last-minute phone call just as we are leaving our office.

My experience actually has been that such calls turn out to be some of the most important ones we get. It could be a novel idea to imagine each time that it is God calling.

Such awareness is a blending of the *doing* and the *being* aspects of our lives, our Martha and Mary parts. Perhaps at times we are called into a state of *being;* and at other times we're led to concentrate on *doing.* I think Williams is asking us to consider both states as offerings to God.

I wonder if Jesus' story of his visit to Mary and Martha would have been different if Martha had believed her *doing* was just as important, but not *more* important, than Mary's *being?*

Buechner, Tillich: Ocean

"They say that whenever the theologian Paul Tillich went to the beach, he would pile up a mound of sand and sit on it gazing out at the ocean with tears running down his cheeks. ...Maybe what made him weep was how vast and overwhelming it was and yet at the same time as near as the breath of it in his nostrils, as salty as his own tears."—Frederick Buechner in *Beyond Words* (HarperOne, 2009).

I share Tillich's awe every time I go to the ocean or the Gulf. It is an experience of both vastness and closeness with Nature and with some Power greater than ourselves. Today I also think about how destructive the sea can be, as I say prayers for friends on the North Carolina coast who were devastated by Hurricane Florence. I remember well the vast destruction along the Gulf of Mexico after hurricanes Frederick, Ivan, Katrina, and Michael.

I also think of the pleasure that the sea and the sand have brought to generations. The sound of the waves calms my soul. Watching children swim and play in the sand pulls at the heartstrings of the child within me. Watching families, lovers, children walk the surf is a lesson in our connectedness to each other. The dolphins, the pelicans, the lone osprey are a constant reminder of the varieties of coexistent life with agendas that differ from our own. The "turtle people" who walk the beach in the early morning looking for turtle tracks to secret nests are, to me, icons of faithfulness and caring about something other than the self.

I see the ocean, the sea, the Gulf, the sand as icons of something created out of love, no matter what the process was.

Living by the sea is like being in a loving relationship with spouse, friend, children. Whenever we take the chance of offering ourselves, our love, to another, it can be beautiful beyond words, like the sea.

Living on the Gulf, we are open to storms—sometimes as ugly and powerful as this hurricane. But like the people I observe by the sea, we remember that the positive potential of love many times overwhelms the possible hurtful negative. The lows are pale compared to the highs. We keep on picking up the mess and forgive the wind and the sea and those we love and hope they can likewise forgive us for the harm we have knowingly or unknowingly done to them.

Nouwen: Our Twilight Zone

"There is a twilight zone in our own hearts that we ourselves cannot see. Other people, especially those who love us, can often see our twilight zones better than we ourselves can. The way we are seen and understood by others is different from the way we see and understand ourselves."—Henri Nouwen in *Bread for the Journey* (HarperSanFrancisco, 1997).

I believe it is not a coincidence that certain people come into our lives. I remember Catherine Marshall talking about praying for patience; and soon afterwards she hired the slowest housekeeper. I learned about homosexuality from so many gay friends, especially Richard and Terry and Joe, as I walked beside them through their struggles. I realized the depth, love, and concern for others present in those of the Muslim faith among my radiology residents and partners, especially Sadaf and her family.

These are all people I already loved. Today I am getting just a slight hint that I also have much to learn from the "difficult" people who come into my path. Over and over I know I am being taught by them about forgiveness; for I know if I cannot forgive the harm they have brought to my life, I continue to let them hurt me. Slowly I also am admitting my part: my character defects, my sins, my hubris, my self-centeredness that contributed to the troublesome situation.

As I meet with friends for spiritual direction, we often discuss what lessons we believe God is teaching us in our contact with each person with whom our lives intersect—whether it be a joyful or difficult experience. Again, this is how we gain the courage to deal with that twilight zone in ourselves and in others that Nouwen describes.

The sacred place where God heals us is in our solidarity—especially as we enlarge our community and take down fences and walls.

August 14: Jonathan Daniels Pilgrimage

"I knew then that I must go to Selma. The Virgin's song was to grow more and more dear in the weeks ahead."—Jonathan Daniels, quoted in *The Jon Daniels Story*, William J. Schneider, ed. (The Seabury Press, 1967), p. 67.

On the second Saturday in August, people from all over the country will be assembling at 11:00 a.m. in Hayneville, Lowndes Country, Alabama, to remember the death of an Episcopal seminarian, Jonathan Myrick Daniels. Daniels died on August 20, 1965, as he was protecting an African American teenage girl named Ruby Sales.

The pilgrimage starts at the courthouse, where a trial lasting less than an hour found the man who murdered Daniels "not guilty." It moves to the place where previously there stood a small country store in which Jonathan was shot. The pilgrimage then moves back to the courthouse for Eucharist, where the bread and the wine are consecrated on an altar that had previously been the judge's bench for that 1965 sham trial.

Bishop Russell Kendrick of the Diocese of Central Gulf Coast reminded us last year that this march remembering the death of the twenty-six-year-old Daniels took place on the same day as the recent disastrous march of white supremacists in Charlottesville, Virginia. The similarities are sometimes too much to bear, reminding us we seem to be no further advanced in race relations than we were three quarters of a century ago. As a nation, we are seriously lacking in our securing of human rights. We all need continued growth in recognizing who is our neighbor.

Daniels took a leave from Episcopal Seminary in Cambridge, Massachusetts, after he heard Martin Luther King, Jr., call for students to join him in his march in Selma, Alabama, to support the Civil Rights movement. He had been moved by singing the *Song of Mary*, the *Magnificat*, in Evening Prayer, and especially by the words: "He hath put down the mighty from their seat and exalted the humble and meek."

Jon devoted many of his Sundays in Selma to bringing small groups of black high school students to services to integrate the local Episcopal church. They were seated but scowled at. Many parishioners openly resented their presence and put their priest squarely and uncomfortably in the middle of the controversy.

In May, Jon went back to seminary to take examinations and complete other requirements. In July he returned to Alabama, where he helped to create a list of helpful local, state, and federal agencies, along with other supportive resources legally available to persons of color.

On Friday, August 13, Jon and others went to the town of Fort Deposit to join in picketing three local businesses. On Saturday they all were arrested and held in the county jail in Hayneville for six days before receiving bail. After their release on Friday, August 20, four of them went to purchase sodas at a local country store, and were met at the door by a special county deputy with a shotgun who told them to leave or be shot. After a brief confrontation, the part-time deputy aimed the gun at a seventeen-year-old black girl in the party, Ruby Sales. Jon pushed her out of the way, took the bullet, and was killed instantly.

Ruby went on to attend the same seminary as Daniels and now heads the SpiritHouse Project in Atlanta, a program using art, spirituality, and education to bring about racial economic and social justice.

Our associate rector, Michael, reminded me that at the School of Theology, Sewanee, Tennessee, during seminary orientation, all the first-year students are loaded into a bus and taken on the Jonathan Daniels pilgrimage. He describes it as a very moving experience for many who are visiting the site of a martyr for the first time.

When we sing or say together *Mary's song,* the *Magnificat (Book of Common Prayer,* p. 119), let us remember Jonathan Myrick Daniels and Ruby Sales and how this Canticle altered both of their lives. Is there something in that song that resonates with each of us as well?

Daniels died on August 20, but is remembered on the day of his arrest, August 14.

Merton: Third Step Prayer

"My Lord God, I have no idea where I am going. I do not see the road ahead of me. Nor do I really know myself, and the fact that I think that I am following your will does not mean that I am actually doing so. But I believe that the desire to please you does in fact please you. ...And I know that if I do this you will lead me by the right road though I may know nothing about it. Therefore will I trust you always though I may seem to be lost.

—Thomas Merton in *Thoughts in Solitude* (1956).

I share many prayers with spiritual friends, and this is one of my favorites. I especially love to pray it along with friends discerning how to become the person God created them to be: when deciding on a vocation, making life-changing decisions, or just trying to live in the present, one day at a time.

This prayer has similarities to the Third Step Prayer (p. 63 in *Alcoholics Anonymous: The Big Book):* "God, I offer myself to Thee—to build with me and do with me as Thou wilt. Relieve me of the bondage of self, that I may better do Thy will. Take away my difficulties, that victory over them may bear witness to those I would help of Thy Power, Thy Love, and Thy Way of Life. May I do Thy will always."

Both of these are prayers of surrender to each day, to whatever God puts in front of us each day.

Guest Writer: Gary Kimmel

"The rhythm of the turns flowed into me as I found my pace and walked where the path would take me."—Twylla Alexander in *Labyrinth Journeys: 50 States, 51 Stories* (Springhill, 2017).

This evening we walked the labyrinth in memory of Les Hunton, a wonderful friend, a fellow singer in the bass section, and a person who always presented a positive attitude. We will miss him. Each time I walk the labyrinth, I come away with different thoughts. Tonight, the labyrinth blessed me with the following:

- The paths we follow are a mixture of short, medium, and long. We spend most of our busy lives on short paths: going to the grocery, taking kids to school, getting over a cold. But some are much longer: taking an extended journey, dealing with a terminal illness. We can walk fast or slow, but we can't avoid these different paths. It is our challenge to focus on the path we are on, not on the path we just left or the one coming up.

- Those who are also on their journey are not always on the same path I am. They may be on a path of a different length; or if they are on the same path, ahead or behind me. Consequently, they may not appreciate where I am in my journey and vice versa. I need to guard against judging their journey based on mine.

- My path is not better or worse than another's. They will be different at a point in time, but not better or worse. All of us will walk these paths, but each of us will be affected in unique ways.

- Richard Rohr points out that there are two stages of life: the building of the ego and the incorporation of that ego into Creation. Likewise, as you enter the labyrinth, you must work a little to come into a contemplative mood. As you walk toward the center, this mood becomes more a part of you. But when you reach the center, you are only halfway. At some point you turn, retrace your steps in a fully contemplative mood, and leave the labyrinth with a new/renewed perspective.

I look forward to my next journey through the labyrinth and what it will bring me.

—Gary Kimmel

Our Neighbor

"The hardest spiritual work in the world is to love the neighbor as the self—to encounter another human being not as someone you can use, change, fix, help, save, enroll, convince or control, but simply as someone who can spring you from the prison of yourself, if you will allow it."—Barbara Brown Taylor in *An Altar in the World: A Geography of Faith* (HarperOne. 2010).

Our older son takes his daughter to high school each day on his way to work. If they have some extra time, they stop at their favorite coffee or smoothie haunt and have a cup of coffee or hot chocolate or smoothie together. I am thinking what a treasure it can be to have a few minutes a day with one of your parents, and maybe even share a cup of your favorite comfort drink. They are both introverts, so they may not say much; but each offers the other a presence in this one-on-one experience, and a chance to get to know each other a little better.

I grew up in a small town with amazing neighbors. Mrs. Rick, a widow with pearl-white hair, lived across the street in a house that seemed huge at the time. One of our neighbors on Second Street had to move away for physical reasons. Mrs. Rick then started walking at 9:00 every morning for seven blocks from Second Street to Ninth Street, up to Riddle's Drug Store, to meet this neighbor for coffee. Our next-door neighbor, Paul, cut Mrs. Rick's grass every week.

I have a friend who calls me every morning. Most people are too busy working to call or talk to one person a day regularly and realize it as a pure gift.

These are the kinds of relationships that work best to "spring" us from ourselves. We don't have to pretend anymore. If we allow such intimacy, these people are permitted to learn who we really are. When we are with them we begin to let down our mask and start becoming the person God created us to be.

Jones: Spiritual Direction and Doubt

"The opposite of faith is not doubt, but certainty."—Alan Jones.

I first heard this quote attributed to Alan Jones, former dean of Grace Cathedral, San Francisco, at a Trinity Wall Street conference at Kanuga in 2001. It warmed my heart when I heard Jones affirm this, and I have shared it with so many others since. Anne Lamott is also a writer and speaker to whom many attribute the quote. Theological friends tell me it is actually from Paul Tillich's work, *Systematic Theology*, Vol. 1, pp. 116-117! I will stop here at tracking it down; but I am certain the sentence is scriptural in its wisdom as well. I share it with so many who come for spiritual direction regarding their doubts.

Jones, in his book, *Soul Making: The Desert Way of Spirituality*, writes about doubt and the finding and nurturing of the soul according to the spirituality of the Desert Fathers. The spirituality of the desert involves encountering God; but subsequently feeling God's absence; and then experiencing the divine joy of God's presence again. Jones describes this threefold experience of soul making after an awakening with the first conversion that entails self-knowledge, often with tears; the second conversion, in which things seem to fall apart; and the third conversion, that occurs when we enter the life of contemplation.

These awakening periods have recurred for me at so many times along the way: at church camps; when I suddenly decided to go to medical school; during my discernment process for the diaconate; and at Cursillo..The conversion of self-knowledge with tears came to me, and the falling apart, when I decided my only hope was to enter a 12-step program. It also came when people close to me: my grandfather, my mother, my father, and my brother died—and it applies now, as my mobility becomes more and more limited.

Often only at the death of a loved one do we recognize the nature of genuine love. Jones describes the tears that come as *like the breaking of waters of the womb before the birth of a child*. The task of love as it is experienced in the "desert" is to free us of our well-built-up exoskeleton.

Soul making is paying attention to things invisible that do not lend themselves to manipulation and control. It requires receptivity to the life of the mystic rather than being the problem solver. Too often we instead spend most of our energy building up our frail ego by setting before it dozens and dozens of minor situations—while the life of the soul is aborted. If the world is to change, then we must change first; and that happens when we live more deeply into our questions and doubts. Sharing our doubt can sometimes bring us together more effectively than sharing our faith, as our faith then eventually becomes stronger. It is a paradox.

The True Prophet

"How do we tell the false prophet from the true prophet? The true prophet seldom predicts the future. The true prophet warns us of our present hardness of heart, our prideful presuming to know God's mind. The final test of the true prophet is love. A mark of the true prophet in any age is humility, self-emptying so there is room for God's Word.—Madeleine L'Engle in *A Stone for a Pillow* (Shaw Books, 2000).

We owe so much to Madeleine L'Engle and her books for children—which are even better for adults. Perhaps what I will remember the most, however, is the fact that her award-winning 1963 Newbery selection, *A Wrinkle in Time*, was rejected twenty-six times before it was published and became an instant science fiction classic!

L'Engle is telling us how we recognize authentic prophets and also how we know we are speaking with a prophetic voice. But there is more. I never know with any certainty when I am doing God's will at the time; but I can sometimes realize afterwards that something was God's will.

L'Engle's thoughts can be helpful here. If my action is all about me, I must ponder if this is really God's will. We are most likely to hear the voice of God when we are in a place of humility, of self-emptying. If an action of mine is done in love or flows from love, that is a good sign that it may express God's will. But Madeleine L'Engle is telling us most of all that if we think we are doing God's will—especially if we feel pride that we are on the right track—we need to stop and reconsider.

So, it's a grand mystery. If we think we have it, we don't. If we don't think we have it, we may. I keep remembering that previous helpful quote: "The opposite of faith is not doubt, but certainty."

To the Joyful Ones

"Shield the joyous; and all for your love's sake."—Order of Compline, *The Book of Common Prayer* (Church Publishing, Inc.), p. 134.

"The joyous." I know these people. I have worked with them. I live with them. I go to the symphony with them. I read their postings on Facebook. They call me in the early morning on the way to work every day. I go to church with them. I serve with them.

I especially find them at one place I never suspected, at our church's weekly Food Pantry.

They are not only the joyful people who serve there, but they are the people who come once a month for food. That is why I selfishly go, not necessarily to offer light, but to receive it, especially from the neediest families. I sit and ask them how they are doing. "I am blessed," is their response. They bring each other to the Food Pantry and talk about how they will share the meals together.

They share poignant stories of how God has been working in their lives, caring for them. They have never met a stranger. They ask us how we have been doing since we last met. Their voices echo laughter. They ask for prayers for other family members. They are teaching us how to live.

Anne Frank: The Remedy

"The best remedy for those who are afraid, lonely or unhappy, is to go outside, somewhere where they can be quite alone with the heavens, nature and God."—From *Anne Frank: The Diary of a Young Girl* (1947).

Anne Frank lived in hiding in a cramped, secret upstairs annex of an office building for over two years with her parents, sister, and four other Jewish people: Hermann and Auguste van Pels, their son Peter, and Fritz Pfeffer. The building was owned by Otto Frank's company, and a bookcase concealed the entrance. Anne and the seven other people could never venture outside. A small window in the attic through which she could see a chestnut tree was her only chance of getting fresh air. In a powerful reflection in her diary, she calls it "the remedy."

Anne was fifteen when her family was discovered and sent to Auschwitz death camp, and later to Bergen-Belsen concentration camp, where she died weeks before British soldiers liberated the camp.

Today we give thanks for the life of Miep Gies, one of Mr. Frank's employees, who helped the Frank family hide and later retrieved Anne's diary. Otto was the only member to survive. He received the diary from Gies on returning to Amsterdam after the liberation.

Every day I know that I take Anne's "remedy," the world outside my window, for granted. I am putting Anne's picture on my desk, hoping to honor her brief life and its truth.

Unlearning and Climbing Down Ladders

"When C. G. Jung was an old man, one of his students read John Bunyan's *Pilgrim's Progress* and asked Jung, 'What has your pilgrimage been?' Jung answered: ' *Pilgrim's Progress* consisted in my having to climb down a thousand ladders until I could reach out my hand to the little clod of earth that I am.'" —*C. G. Jung Letters,* Vol. 1, Gerhard Adler and Aniela Jaffé, eds. (Routledge & Kegan Paul, 1972), p. 19, footnote 8.

Richard Rohr describes the spiritual path of unlearning and climbing down as "The way down is the way up." We spend our lives learning and unlearning, climbing up and climbing down. Thomas Merton said, "People may spend their entire lives climbing the ladder of success only to find, when they reach the top, that the ladder is leaning against the wrong building."

When three spiritual leaders share this secret, I listen. My experience is that people who try to stay at the top of the ladder soon are overtaken by younger and smarter people in their profession. Attempting to contend with this paradox leads many people to seek spiritual direction. They realize that their old life no longer holds the answers. Their soul cries out to be heard.

The "climb down" can be gentle, with the help of our friends who care for us *because they love us,* not due to what we have accomplished. They see the face of Christ in us and try to describe it to us. We meet some fascinating people on the way down whom we never would have paid attention to before. The outer life becomes less important. Our inner life speaks more clearly and becomes heard. The descent is an ascent.

Richard Rohr, *Simplicity: The Freedom of Letting Go* (Crossroad Publishing, 2003), pp. 168-169, 172-173.

Charleston: Gladness, Gratefulness, Acceptance, Peace

"Be glad today for the many small graces that line the path of our lives like flowers. Be open to the surprises that may come and alert to the quiet messages whispered on the wind. Be creative in how you shape your life in these few hours for every day is a blank canvas. Be a blessing to others as the night draws near and let your evening prayers keep them safe until you awake again."—Bishop Steven Charleston Daily Facebook Page.

Every day we have choices. First, we can obsess over the past, what we have lost, mistakes we have made. Second, we can obsess over the future, what we will lose, especially as we age or fall into new mistakes. The past and the potential future become our "gods, taking up rent in our heads"—consuming all our time and energy. Our mind keeps racing faster to make plans and find solutions.

Our third choice is living consciously, moment by moment, in the now. We can enjoy, treasure, give thanks for the gifts of each day, what comes to us in each present moment. This involves an impressive of awareness of our surroundings and of our relationships, enlarging our worldview, getting "out of ourselves." The challenge is not to forget the mistakes we have made, but to learn from them so we can make them less frequently in the future.

Acceptance of ourselves as works in progress, not works seeking perfection, is huge. Acceptance that there is a power greater than ourselves caring for us is paramount. I daily talk with people who were upset about plans that were not going their way, only to become thankful later, because "their plan" would have been destructive.

I think of old boyfriends I obsessed about who ignored me as a teenager. I realize today that my life would have been a disaster with any of them. I think of people who came and continue to come into my life to change its direction when I am going the wrong way. I think of people who cared for our children when we couldn't or were not the ones they needed at the time.

As we age, we may find ourselves filled with anxiety from contemplating deterioration of health, the death of a spouse, or living on a fixed income. There are so many uncertainties.

We have a part to play in overcoming this. We need to do our best to keep ourselves healthy through diet and exercise and proper medical care. But then our best response should be to wake up each morning with gratitude for the gifts of another day together.

Acceptance and gratitude are our cornerstones, the major building blocks to peace and serenity. I am writing this so I will continue to believe it.

Cameron: The Artist's Way

"Do not call procrastination laziness. Call it fear. Fear is what blocks an artist. The fear of not being good enough. The fear of not finishing. The fear of failure and of success. The fear of beginning at all. There is only one cure for fear. That cure is love. Use love for your artist to cure its fear. Stop yelling at yourself. Be nice. Call fear by its right name."—Julia Cameron in *The Artist's Way: A Spiritual Path to Higher Creativity* (Tarcher, 1995).

When I suggest to friends that they should consider writing as a spiritual practice, most respond that they don't know how to start, or they have no talent as a writer. It is not their gift. The best antidote to this fear of writing or fear of inadequacy as a writer is Julia Cameron's book, *The Artist's Way*. Cameron suggests starting to write by rising in the morning and writing "morning pages," which she calls the "primary tool of creative recovery." These are three longhand pages of whatever comes into our mind. These reflections do not have to make "sense." Writing them is intended to be a listening exercise in the morning: imagining that it is the hand of God moving through our hand as we write.

I have also experienced this exercise as a clearing or cleaning out of the garbage in my head. Fearful thoughts stay powerful when they remain in my head; but when I put them on paper, some of their power over me goes away. Perhaps in some way I am turning them over, releasing them to God, so that the creative process can begin.

Cameron recommends that every night we pray for guidance and ask for answers. The morning pages are a process of listening for the answers as the day begins.

I often write on the inside covers of books the date when I started reading them. As I reread Cameron's book, I pull back her cover and see a date twenty years ago. Memories flood in of the book group at St. Margaret's Episcopal Church with which I read *The Artist's Way* over one summer. I especially remember Lee Nix, who had been the chair of my discernment committee, who was a mentor to me, an encourager of creativity.

I believe it enhances the experience to read, write, and work through a book like *The Artist's Way* with a book study group—to go together through the book's many suggested activities and exercises. Today I am reminded also of how powerful just writing down a date can be in the context of spiritual writing.

Cymbals and Morning Prayer

"Praise him with loud clanging cymbals!"—Psalm 150:5.

I frequently read Morning Prayer online from *The Daily Office* (dailyoffice.wordpress.com) posted by Josh Thomas in Indiana. Josh calls the site "not a website but a community" because an interactive Morning Prayer is offered during the week online and as a webcast at 7:00 and 9:00 in the mornings. There is also a video Evensong every Friday night at 9:00. Josh, who founded dailyoffice.org in 2004, is a vicar and lay commission evangelist in the Episcopal Church. I am drawn to the website because of the ease of reading Morning Prayer according to the tradition of *The Book of Common Prayer;* but I especially look forward to the artwork, the music, and short related discussions Josh and his staff bring to the Daily Office.

Recently Josh included some information about cymbals in worship, referencing this article in the *New York Times* by Lara Pellegrinelli with a photograph by Kayana Szymczak:

https://www.nytimes.com/2018/08/03/arts/music/zildjian-cymbals-400-years.html

For over 400 years, an Armenian family has been manufacturing what is considered the world's best cymbal, called Zildjian, which means in Armenian, "son of the cymbal maker." The family first developed the cymbal for the Sultan of Turkey but moved the business to Massachusetts just before the Armenian genocide. The cymbals are made from a carefully guarded family secret alloy of tin, copper, and silver, and the company is today led by its fourteenth generation of cymbal makers and the first female CEO, Craigne Zildjian.

We sometimes have cymbals in our resurrection Easter worship; but we more often see them used in bands and at the symphony. Interestingly, no two cymbals are exactly alike.

Today I learned about an instrument we so often see and hear, but take for granted, and one we would normally not consider interesting unless we were drummers or percussionists. I learned that this powerful instrument came alive 400 years ago when an Armenian artisan convinced a Sultan that the cymbal would be a significant instrument to mark the rhythmic cycles each morning before prayer, and every evening after prayer.

Next time I am at the symphony I will pay more attention to the cymbal player and give thanks for this Armenian family that has made a difference in so many of our lives.

The Zildjian family story is only one of so many powerful stories to be told about people who have come to this country seeking a new life, and who have enriched all our lives in ways we most often take for granted.

Addiction and Spiritual Direction

"We have entered into the world of the Spirit. Our next function is to grow in understanding and effectiveness. This is not an overnight matter. It should continue for our lifetime."—*The Big Book of Alcoholics Anonymous,* 4th edition (Alcoholics Anonymous World Services, 2001), p. 84.

Sometimes those coming to me for spiritual direction are blocked because of addiction. They have filled their "God hole" with another form of spirit, alcohol or drugs, and this is no longer working. How do we help spiritual friends who need recovery? First, as you know, this is a disease, not a moral failing. And denial is an ENORMOUS part of the disease. It is the only disease that tells you that *you do not have the disease;* so, look for subtle hints. If this comes up, it could be a time to suggest the name of a therapist specializing in addiction, or a best friend of the person in a recovery program. People in recovery will tell a listener their story—what it was like when they were drinking, and now what their life is like in a recovery or 12-step program. This should become a two-way street. Telling their story keeps them sober as well as possibly helping someone else. I know of no more powerful act of love than being vulnerable enough to tell someone else your story about how another, a new Spirit, has entered your life and made all the difference.

Most people do not understand how spiritual 12-step programs are. They offer an alternative way of life, a road less traveled. Statistics say that only about ten percent of people with alcohol addiction make it to recovery. Recovery is not just about not drinking; it provides an entirely fresh perspective: looking at and relating to the world with a new pair of glasses. Alcohol might have been a way to cope with living life on life's terms. After we stop drinking, we will need an alternative coping mechanism, which is a relationship with a higher power that most call God.

I remember, when I first started going to a 12-step program, that I soon believed it would be impossible for me to recover, after I was told that the heart of this program was spiritual. I already was a very spiritual person, leading groups, writing articles about faith! However, I soon realized that God was a *part* of my life, but *I* was in charge—the pilot; and I gave God the position of copilot, being there to help me with my plans. I had been told this in church since an early age: to put *God* in charge of my life. But I had to hear it someplace else to develop the incentive to change—for I have such magnificent ideas!

Charleston: Imagination

"The light under the door to your mind is your imagination. It is always glowing, always searching for a new idea, always alive and energetic. If you want to enlighten your spiritual life, try the one channel of contact to the Spirit that is the most direct: use your imagination. The curious, playful, unlimited vision of what you can imagine is a hint of how the Spirit thinks. It is a point of contact for us because when we open ourselves up to thinking and seeing in new ways, we are stepping into a sacred process. If you want to find the Spirit, open the door."—Bishop Steven Charleston Daily Facebook Page (3/7/2019).

Bishop Charleston affirms that using our imagination is one pathway to connecting to God. My experience is that my prayers are more meaningful if I imagine each of the people I am praying for sitting near me, or holding the hand of Jesus or God or the Holy Spirit. I am turning each of them over to our loving God, who is guarding and caring for them.

In the forgiveness prayer from Contemplative Outreach, Ltd., we imagine being with a person who has harmed us. We sit in a safe place, with God beside us, as we tell the person how he or she has hurt us; and then we hope we can say words of forgiveness. This is not a onetime prayer, but a practice we repeat over and over again in our own sacred space until we reach the place of forgiveness—with God by our side.

In Ignatian study of Scripture, we imagine ourselves in the scenes of Jesus' life when he was on earth. We join the crowd following Jesus. We may become the Samaritan woman he meets at noon. We may stand in the crowd at the foot of his cross as he is dying. We may be with the women who first discover he has risen.

In dream work, we practice active imagination by conversing with people and images as they present themselves in our dream. In our imagination, these participants in the dream can tell us who they are and explain to us the parts of *ourselves* that they represent.

Anthony de Mello encourages us to make albums in our imagination of joyful times in our lives. Then we can come back to our album from time to time, especially in troublesome times, to remember what we experienced. De Mello also believes that at the time of a past event we never appreciated its richness. Returning in our minds and actually "getting back" into the scene can bring even greater joy; and we may feel greater love than when an event first happened.

Imagination is one of our best spiritual practices.

Redbud Blossoms and Fig Trees

Then [Jesus] told this parable: "A man had a fig tree planted in his vineyard; and he came looking for fruit on it and found none. So he said to the gardener, 'See here! For three years I have come looking for fruit on this fig tree, and still I find none. Cut it down! Why should it be wasting the soil?' He replied, 'Sir, let it alone for one more year, until I dig around it and put manure on it. If it bears fruit next year, well and good; but if not, you can cut it down.'"—Luke 13:6-9.

There is a wild redbud tree outside my office window that in the spring had beautiful pink budding flower clusters very close to the stem. The tree is in the middle of a line of wild bushes and hardwood trees. For several years I saw no new life on it. Then, one spring, I noticed these beautiful blossoms and wondered where they were coming from.

When I went back to my office, I could not find the tree. Then I looked up from my desk. There they were, high above the other trees. The tree was flowering only in the canopy above my window. Lower down in my direct vision there were no blossoms. It gave me pause, and I determined to stop during the day to look up from my line of vision—to interrupt my work to glance away and take in the beauty of the blossoms.

One more lesson from my blossoming redbud tree: Very near its trunk, it has divided into three parts. For years, it looked as though only one division was living and flowering. The other two large sections had no leaves or blossoms. Then, this year, I notice that at the very top of the middle division, clusters of blossoms have formed.

I am reminded of the fig tree in the Gospels. Jesus calls us to be patient and expectant. What is difficult to detect and may *seem* to be dead may still be very much alive and capable of producing beauty and fruit.

Carver: Gravy

"No other word will do. For that's what it was.
Gravy.
Gravy, these past ten years.
Alive, sober, working, loving, and
being loved by a good woman. Eleven years
ago he was told he had six months to live
at the rate he was going. And he was going
nowhere but down. So he changed his ways
somehow. He quit drinking! And the rest?
After that it was all gravy, every minute
of it, up to and including when he was told about
well, some things that were breaking down and
building up inside his head. 'Don't weep for me.'
he said to his friends. 'I'm a lucky man.
I've had ten years longer than I or anyone
expected. Pure Gravy. And don't forget it.'"

—Raymond Carver in *New Yorker* (9/29/1988), p. 28.

It is not unusual that people coming for spiritual direction are seeking some relief from an addiction. They are under the influence of another "spirit" and have "seen through a glass darkly" that the answer may be a spiritual one—a relationship with what those in recovery call "a higher power." They may just come for a brief time. As a spiritual friend, we are there to care for their soul that has been anesthetized, put to sleep by drugs, alcohol, work, shopping, etc. We keep looking to see where God has been working in the person's life, caring for that soul; and we keep praying that through those moments he or she will know God's leading to the world of Spirit.

There is a recovery theme or principle that a person caught in addiction must reach some kind of "bottom" before he or she will have a moment of clarity leading to a desire to change. We look for that bottom and hope to bring to awareness what the person can learn from that devastating event or events.

Raymond Carver was a brilliant poet, short story writer—and an alcoholic. When he reached his bottom in June of 1977, he went into recovery for ten years. This is his famous poem about his last ten years in recovery, written at age fifty before he died of lung cancer. It is also inscribed on his tombstone in Port Angeles, Washington. I sometimes share this poem when that moment of clarity comes to someone I am talking with.

Olivia Laing has written an insightful book, *The Trip to Echo Spring* (Picador, 2013), about the association between creativity and alcohol in the lives of six writers: F. Scott Fitzgerald, Ernest Hemingway, Tennessee Williams, John Berryman, John Cheever, and Raymond Carver. Carver is the only one of these six who found significant recovery.

Carver: Recovery

"LATE FRAGMENT
And did you get what
you wanted from this life, even so?
I did.
And what did you want?
To call myself beloved, to feel myself
beloved on the earth."
—Inscription on the tombstone of Raymond Carver along with his poem "Gravy."

This takes me back again to Olivia Laing's story in *The Trip to Echo Spring* on the relationships of six award-winning, but alcohol-addicted, authors: F. Scott Fitzgerald, Ernest Hemingway, Tennessee Williams, John Berryman, John Cheever, and Raymond Carver. Knowing that Carver is the only one of these six majorly talented American writers who went into significant 12-step recovery for any length of time tells us a great deal about addiction—how cunning and baffling the disease is even for the most brilliant and creative of minds.

I hope you have a chance to read my favorite Carver story, "A Small Good Thing" about a dying son, his birthday cake, and the baker of the cake. Make sure you read Carver's original version, published after his death by his wife, Tess Gallagher, in *Beginners* (Vintage, 2015).

For people caught in this disease, their addiction, alcohol, drugs, sex, relationships, work—all become their God, their higher power. It is impossible to find the relationship with God that our life continues to call us to when there is something else in our "God hole." The paradox is that the answer, the awakening, the Lazarus experience for any addiction is a spiritual one: turning our lives and wills over to the care of the God of our understanding.

Buechner, Gandhi: A Telling Silence

"I remember going to see the movie *Gandhi* when it first came out. ... We were the usual kind of noisy, restless Saturday night crowd. But by the time the movie came to a close with the flames of Gandhi's funeral pyre filling the entire wide screen, there was not a sound or a movement in that whole theater, and we filed out of there— teenagers and senior citizens, blacks and whites—in as deep and telling a silence as I have ever been part of."—Frederick Buechner in *The Clown in the Belfry* (HarperCollins, 1992).

We long to silence the busyness in our heads. We try meditation, interacting with children, exercise, being outdoors, or just sitting. Sometimes art forms can move us from our head to our hearts—to the Christ within us—in record time, as in the old Superman slogans, "like a speeding bullet." Movies can do this for me, especially stories of those who know what suffering is and have learned from it rather than choosing to avoid the reality of it. I had the same experience as Buechner and his fellow viewers when I first saw the movie, *Gandhi*. As we by chance might have glanced over at the strangers on either side of us in the packed theater, none of us needed to feel embarrassed by our tears.

We all walked out of the theater in silence. There were no words. The transformative power of this 1982 movie still speaks to us each time we see it, now over thirty years later.

Since today we more often watch movies in our homes than in the theater, we are less likely to experience the powerful community reaction that Buechner and I had.

The movie *Gandhi,* about someone who brought about change by nonviolence, is the story we need to remember every day.

Turning It Over

"I abandon all that I think I am, all that I hope to be, all that I believe I possess. I let go of the past, I withdraw my grasping hand from the future, and in the great silence of this moment, I alertly rest my soul."
—Howard Thurman in *Deep Is the Hunger* (Friends United Press, 1978).

The first line of this quote, "I abandon all that I think I am," reminds me of the exchange of rings in the liturgy of the celebration of a marriage. "*N, I give you this ring as a symbol of my vow, and with all that I am, and all that I have, I honor you, in the Name of God*" *(The Book of Common Prayer,* p. 317). Thurman goes even further than the vow at the exchange of rings. This prayer now turns over to God all that we think we are, all that we might hope to be, all that we imagine we possess: our past, present, and future. The result, in the silence of the moment, is that we mindfully rest into our soul, united to the God within us, and find that peace that words cannot describe.

This is freedom. I am no longer in charge. Doing the next right thing, but not worrying about the results. Each of us striving to be the person God created us to be, not the person others may call us to be. Discerning and then doing what we think we are uniquely called to do. Hoping to find direction through spiritual practices and inner work as we live faithfully in community. Listening. Listening to other people's stories. Then, at the right time, telling our own story. Learning how to forgive and to be forgiven. Being always grateful. Becoming a servant leader.

This is the life of surrender.

Dolphins and Waiting

"So God created the great sea monsters and every living creature that moves, of every kind, with which the waters swarm."—Genesis 1:21.

I wake up too late to see the sun-rising spectacle on the Gulf of Mexico, but it is still quiet with only the blue heron and pelicans and sea gulls stirring about. A lone "Share the Beach" sea turtle volunteer now arrives with her stethoscope to monitor the walled-off clutch of turtle eggs just in front of our condominium. A second turtle volunteer in a green shirt arrives from a different direction. They are conferencing. They think tonight may be the night.

I just want to sit. Something keeps me from checking my email or going over my prepared morning sermon one more time. I just wait. Something tells me to wait.

There are not words to describe what soon happens A white fishing boat motors, then pauses, then motors on the horizon. On either side, in front and behind the boat, are at least five or six dolphins swimming, jumping out of the water beside the boat! My instinct is to yell out to the fishermen to turn off their motors. I don't want the dolphins to get caught in an engine.

Are these dolphins being trained for some aquarium? They follow so closely. The fishermen don't seem to observe the dolphins. This must be old hat to them. I don't see them throwing fish to entice the dolphins to follow the boat. The boat turns around and the dolphins follow, pursuing the boat until it is out of sight.

The sighting was brief but revealed something I had never considered before. I Google "why dolphins follow boats." This may not be an uncommon occurrence, but it was new to me. It is called "bow riding" when dolphins surf in the wave created by boats, and "wake riding" when dolphins swim along and surf in the waves created by the back of boats. Google cannot explain it, but suggests the dolphins are just playing and enjoying the surf. What a novel idea. Nature is affirming our need to play.

Later at church I talk to our old friend Chan, who knows all about the sea. She thinks the fishing boat probably was a shrimp trawler, and that after gathering the shrimp, the fishermen throw the rest of the sea's treasure back. It becomes a feast for dolphins. Dolphins have learned instinctively to follow these boats and wait for the catch of the day. So the dolphin show could have been related to food rather than fun—but could it be both?

That evening at sunset I sit again in silence. I keep thinking about how I was instinctively able that morning to sit by the sea and wait and watch for the dolphins instead of getting caught up in the agenda for the day. Synchronicity, serendipity: the occurrence of events that appear significantly related. Now I don't know if my expectancy was related to the dolphin spectacle that unfolded; but I am staying open, especially to more sitting and waiting and watching by the sea.

King: The Great Stumbling Block

"I have almost reached the regrettable conclusion that the Negro's great stumbling block in the stride toward freedom is not the White Citizen's Councilor or Ku Klux Klanner, but the white moderate more devoted to 'order' than to justice; who prefers a negative peace which is the absence of tension to a positive peace of justice; who says, 'I agree with you in the goal you seek, but I can't agree with your methods of direct action;' who paternalistically feels he can set the timetable for another man's freedom; who lives by the myth of time and who constantly advises the Negro to wait until a 'more convenient season.'"—Martin Luther King, Jr., "Letter from Birmingham Jail," April 16, 1963.

I repeat part of the message from MLK this morning, for this letter from jail still speaks so profoundly to us in another century. We live in a time of paradox that continually shuttles us between "be patient" and "time to act." How do we know which to do? I think part of MLK's message is that what is a "more convenient season" for one, is not so for another. Most of us do not understand what it has been like to walk in the shoes of those who have been oppressed for years, even centuries. I also know that in my life, if I wait for the "most convenient time," that time will never be, never happen.

When is the most convenient time to get married, have children, tell the truth, visit the sick, go to church, write, read, go on vacation, retire? I remember what a friend early in my recovery said at a 12-step meeting many, many years ago: "I am all right as long as I have all my ducks in a row." Well, my experience is that those ducks never perfectly line up in a row! There is always some inconvenience that will keep us and our ducks in disarray and prevent us from doing any of the things we know are right and that we feel called to do.

We try to find "the most convenient time" to pray, meditate, be silent. There is always some reason that something else should be done instead, especially marking off the other things on our to-do list for the day.

We are called to "make time" for these things by deciding on priorities. We know this, but the doing is the hard part. We want to thank MLK today for putting us in our place, reminding us to listen more carefully to the cries of those who are oppressed, to the parts of ourselves that are oppressed—and to the parts of the needy who come for spiritual direction. We are called to *listen, listen, listen,* and to reach out, even at a most inconvenient time.

Starting Schools and Dolphins and Turtles

"We are tied to the ocean. And when we go back to the sea, whether it is to sail or to watch —we are going back from whence we came."—John F. Kennedy.

I arise early before dawn and watch the world come alive on the sea. The Gulf is smooth with almost no waves. Its appearance is more like a glassy lake than the roaring ocean. It is so calm, I can see schools of fish moving rhythmically near the shore. There are more dolphins than I have ever seen before. They are swimming to my right, to the left, in the water in front of the condo. The large mammals move like ballet dancers in slow motion, with poise and confidence. Schools of fish. Schools of dolphins.

I think of two years ago when my two granddaughters both started new schools, one beginning college, the other starting high school. I want to send them love for their exciting adventures. I think most of us can still remember our first college class, our first day of high school. Could all of nature also be celebrating these new journeys with my granddaughters and all others starting unknown adventure this early morning? I will just take it as a potential sign that generates warmth in my heart to send on to them.

My husband goes down to the beach to talk to a gathering of turtle volunteers about the turtle nest in front of our condo. There are tracks from at least one of the clutch that wobbled down to the sea last night. More turtle people arrive and wait for what they call "the boil," when the rest of the 120 turtles hatch. Today, perhaps 119 turtles will start a new journey, just like Langley and Zoe.

I am overwhelmed about our ability to feel and send connection to the world around us, to nature, and to those we so dearly love who are physically removed from us. I still feel this connection to my grandparents that began so many years ago.

Today all the world as far as I can see seems to affirm love and connection and new beginnings.

Buechner, Ignatius: News of the Day

"When the evening news comes on, hundreds of thousands of people all over the earth are watching it on their TV screens. There is also the news that rarely gets into the media, and that is the news of each particular day of each particular one of us. Maybe there's nothing on earth more important for us to do than sit down every evening and think it over, try to figure it out, at least try to come to terms with it. The news of our day. It is, if nothing else, a way of saying our prayers."—Frederick Buechner.

Buechner here challenges us to spend even a fraction of the time that we spend listening to the *world* news of the day, dealing with the news *in our own life*. In fact, 12-step groups, short courses in Christianity such as Cursillo, and Ignatian spirituality all suggest methods for reviewing the day, giving thanks, making gratitude lists, thinking back to when we encountered God, when we harmed ourselves or others, asking for forgiveness, planning to make amends, and in essence *turning our life and our will over to God* one more time each evening. Those in recovery call it the 10th step. St. Ignatius calls it the Examen.

Buechner reminds us we should consider these exercises as prayer. It is our news of the day for God, nighttime news, nighttime prayers. In time, answers will come as to how we are to respond to the world news of the day.

Sabbath

"Sabbath-keeping is a resistance movement, and it's very counter-cultural. Sabbath-keeping is a resistance to the clutter, the noise, the advertising, the busyness, and the 'virtual living' that sucks the life out of our lives. Sabbath-keeping is a resistance to constant production, and work, and accumulation. It may be the most difficult of the Ten Commandments to keep, and it may also be the most important."—Br. Curtis Almquist, SSJE, from "Brother, Give Us a Word," a daily email sent to friends and followers of the Society of Saint John the Evangelist (SSJE.org).

Keeping Sabbath in our culture is more than difficult. I have one friend who rests completely on the Sabbath. She does nothing work-related, trying to spend as much time as possible outdoors. I am reminded of my grandparents, who followed this rule as well. My grandmother would not even do a little sewing on Sunday. I often spent Sundays with them. We ate, we rested, we walked around my grandfather's farm, and we went to church. We watched the *Ed Sullivan Show* at night on the television after making Seven Up floats. I would then spend the night in their guest double bed, which seemed unbelievably huge at the time. I remember most of all the feeling of love and peace on these days. I wonder how much was related to Sabbath-keeping.

They mentored for me how to keep the Sabbath, but I have forgotten. *I am an important person. I will never make those deadlines unless I do a little work on Sunday.* A little turns into several hours' worth. Once I start, it is hard to stop. I will rest later.

I want to keep the Sabbath. It is not too late to start. Join me. Let us encourage one another. Maybe we need a Sabbath recovery group to share stories with each other about what happens when we keep the Sabbath.

When I meet with people to offer spiritual direction, I try to ask them how they keep Sabbath. I am hoping to learn from them as much as to remind them of this spiritual gift, which is also the third commandment. It may be the only spiritual gift that is a commandment.

The Ten Commandments honor God, but also were given for our own health and safety. Sometimes it is helpful for me to view them not just as rules, but as guides to a healthy life—more important than diet and exercise.

God's Presence

"When like Elijah you're surprised by sheer silence, listen to God speaking deep inside. When like Peter you're scared by the wind on the sea, look to Jesus right there with you. When bedtime nears, stop and review how the Spirit caught you by the hand and caught you off guard with love. Hold these close to your heart and go to sleep."— Br. Luke Ditewig, SSJE, from "Brother, Give Us a Word," a daily email sent to friends and followers of the Society of Saint John the Evangelist (SSJE.org).

God's promise is that God is always with us, beside us. Always. All the time. How do we feel that presence? My experience is that when I am connected to the God within me, the Christ within me, and when I can see the God, the Christ, in my neighbor, I am feeling God's presence.

When we feel the fruit of the Spirit, love, joy, peace, patience, generosity, gentleness, faithfulness, self-control, and kindness (Galatians 5:22-23), we are feeling God's presence. When suddenly we realize we were able to do something we did not think we were up to doing, we are feeling God's presence.

During troublesome times, God shows up in the presence of someone who loves us just as we are. This epiphany can take the form of a phone call, an email, a snail mail, or even a text.

It is difficult to spend any time outdoors in nature or even to look outdoors to see the birds feeding near our windows without feeling the presence of something greater than myself.

Gratitude helps us to put on new glasses so we can see God's presence in our lives.

Forgiving ourselves and others keeps us from putting up the barriers that prevent us from seeing God in our lives.

Beauty in art, music, the sacred word, poetry, fiction, and nonfiction writings can open up our eyes and ears and mind to see God sitting right beside us—on a bench at the National Gallery, or in the center orchestra section, or with us as we're curled up in our favorite chair.

Canoeing the Mountains

"Unless a grain of wheat falls into the earth and dies, it remains just a single grain; but if it dies, it bears much fruit."—John 12:24.

A recent *Alban Weekly* from Duke Divinity School interviews Tod Bolsinger,[1] professor at Fuller Theological Seminary, about the meaning of the title of his recent book, *Canoeing the Mountains: Christian Leadership in Uncharted Territory* (IVP Books, 2018).

Bolsinger provides us with an amazing metaphor for so many of our transition experiences in life. He tells the story of the journey of the explorers Lewis and Clark, who thought when they reached the Continental Divide, they would find a navigable river leading directly to the Pacific Ocean. Instead, they met the Rocky Mountains.

They didn't survive by trying to canoe the mountain. And they didn't let this obstacle destroy their objective. They had to adapt; and their key to survival came from a source of wisdom that was not part of their hierarchy or privilege.

I think what Bolsinger is trying to tell our churches can apply to aspects of our own life. We have so much to learn from people who know what it is like to reach the top of a mountain with a canoe in hand and yet accomplish what seems at the time to be an unsurmountable task. These survivors have a sense of a GPS calling them back home. Immigrants, people of color, and women especially have had to adapt to overwhelming situations, and their experiences have much to teach us. More and more we are called to listen to their stories.

Lewis and Clark encountered the needed wisdom from a teenager, a nursing mother, a Native American who was kidnapped as a child. "She wasn't in unfamiliar terrain; she was going home." Bolsinger reminds us that transformation most often comes from loss, and those who do not have power may be the true experts in overcoming precarious situations. They may be the best trained in survival and wilderness experiences. Just as Lewis and Clark had to take direction from a young Indian mother, Bolsinger reminds us of the wisdom of *giving up power so that something much greater can be birthed.* This also is a basic premise in recovery programs.

The canoe metaphor is an apt one for our individual life transitions. What mountains on our journey have we encountered, equipped with only a "canoe": an energy useful at one time in our life, but is not the expertise we need now? What does it mean for us to listen more carefully to survivors—survivors in our own world and survivor-parts of our inner world that can guide us along the next pathway?

[1] "Tod Bolsinger: What Does It Mean to Stop Canoeing the Mountains?" *Faith and Leadership, Alban at Duke Divinity School,* alban@div.duke.edu, 8/13/2018.

Nouwen: Trees and Needing Praise

"Trees that grow tall have deep roots. Great height without great depth is dangerous. The great leaders of this world—like St. Francis, Gandhi, and Martin Luther King, Jr.—were all people who could live with public notoriety, influence, and power in a humble way because of their deep spiritual rootedness. Those who are deeply rooted in the love of God can enjoy human praise without being attached to it."— Henri Nouwen in *Bread for the Journey* (HarperSanFrancisco, 1997).

Nouwen gives us an amazing sign of when our connection to God is thin. When we are needing the praise and adoration of others, we are not "rooted" in God. Living off of the praise of others is living on the surface. Needing the positive opinion of others is like a "stop sign."

Stop! We are going in the wrong direction. Turn around. Go and sit or walk outdoors. Recognize that there dwells in nature something greater than ourselves. Remember that a loving God has our welfare so completely in mind that God created all this for us to care for and enjoy.

Talk to a spiritual friend. Do one of the many, many spiritual exercises we most often practice to reconnect to God. Reexamine your rule of life.

Reach out in love to someone else, especially someone in need. Make eye contact. Look for the light of Christ in that person. Connect the Christ in us to the Christ in the other person. I think this is one way that our souls need to extend and enlarge to nurture deeper roots.

Humor

"Laughter is carbonated holiness."—Anne Lamott.

Anne Lamott is a brilliant writer who has helped me look for the humor in the truth.

There is no question that the God of our understanding has a sense of humor. Therefore, our spiritual life or relationship with God also should reflect that humor. Some things that happen to us can be explained only by acknowledging that *our God does indeed have sense of humor!* This is the God who keeps bringing annoying people into my life–until I realize that what bothers me about them is something unrecognized in myself. I see this as an example of God's little "jokes."

Sometimes there are situations in life that can be tolerated only by our having a sense of humor. There was a boy in our medical school class, Mike Levinson, whose frequent quote was, "You've got to laugh or you will cry!" Some challenges then were so difficult that we had to find some lightness in them. When we can acknowledge humor and even absurdity in life, I believe that that is the Spirit working in us to comfort us. *If the joke is at someone else's expense,* making fun of another—it is not from God. I see God in situations when I can see humor in some of my own character defects, my sins. "Goodness gracious, God, I just did it again!"

I learned about humor and character defects from 12-step groups. It is not "gallows humor" when something deadly serious is made fun of in a silly or seemingly disrespectful way. There is a fine line.

My mother did the best she could in her lifetime, but I did not appreciate her. I can now remember that every time I would call her, I would expect *her* to be different, instead of contemplating how I might change *my way of relating to her.* I now look back on this, and rather than beating myself up, I see how humorous it is to "do the same thing over and over the same way and expect a different result." It is so true that it is humorous. It is also insanity!

When I become too serious or am visited by a friend who is looking at life too soberly, my experience is that the antidote for both of us is *play:* playing with our children or grandchildren, being with friends who know better than we do how to lighten up and "let go."

Facebook and First Day of School

"For everything there is a season, and a time for every matter under heaven."—Ecclesiastes 3:1.

I remember this morning how I became engaged on Facebook for almost an hour a couple of months ago! I had gotten up early to post the *Daily Something* and was overwhelmed by the pictures of children going back to school that week. I couldn't stop looking at them. There were children I knew from previous churches; children and grandchildren of people I worked with at Children's Hospital; children I sang and prayed with at the Cathedral School; children from so many Vacation Bible Schools—children I learned from and dearly loved. Some were almost grown.

Most of the younger children and some teenagers agreed to look happy and excited for their parents' pictures. I envision these same photographs brought in albums and embarrassingly shown at future weddings and anniversaries. I think of the joy of grandparents and friends who cannot see their loved ones as often as they would like, but frequently visit with them on Facebook.

"Where have all the years gone?" was an often-quoted heading with the pictures. I agree. Life is so fleeting. That is why living in the moment, the precious present—loving and enjoying the "now"—is so important. I realize I remember these children most because I did, for a nanosecond, stay present with them at some time in the past. Today I send love to each of them. They in turn have sent love back to my heart, as I remember who they were and cherish who they are today.

Anthony de Mello reminds us to keep our album of wonderful memories so we can go back and relive them even more fully than the first time. He believes that often a first encounter is too powerful for us to take in. He encourages us to guard and keep these memories for when we want or need to reconnect to their power in the past.

Living in the present gives us such beautiful, loving memories; but there also is a season for going back to relive those memories. Times of transitions in our lives, such as starting school, can trigger this need.

That was a splendid day on Facebook, worth getting up early to see—and a grand excuse for forgetting to check the regular news of the day.

Remembering September 11: Father Mychal's Prayer

"Lord, take me where you want me to go;

Let me meet who you want me to meet;

Tell me what you want me to say, and

Keep me out of your way. Amen."

—Father Mychal Judge, O. F. M., Chaplain, New York Fire Department, World Trade Center Death Certificate Number 1.

This now-famous prayer of Father Mychal Judge, who died at the World Trade Center on 9/11/2001, was again continually on my mind yesterday during our country's moment of silence. We all paused respectfully as we heard the names read of the almost 3000 people who had died that early autumn morning in four coordinated attacks on this country. Flags were at half-staff as we traveled yesterday.

Mychal Judge, a Franciscan friar and Catholic priest who was serving as a chaplain to the New York City Fire Department, was not afraid to become part of the messiness of life. After the first attack, he prayed over bodies in the streets, and then went into the lobby of the North Tower, which had become an emergency command post. He was killed by flying debris when the South Tower collapsed.

His biographers[1] say that his dying prayer was "Jesus, please end this right now! God, please end this!" The iconic photograph of five men carrying his body out of the North Tower has been described as an American *Pieta,* comparing it to another Michael's statue of Mary holding the dead body of Jesus in St. Peter's, Rome; or to a lesser-known work of Michelangelo, *Deposition with Joseph of*

Arimathea [with thanks to Barbara Crafton for making this connection].

Father Mychal was also appreciatively remembered as a staunch supporter of LGBT rights, and as a sober member of Alcoholic Anonymous for twenty-three years. Another 3000 people were reported to have attended his funeral. Father Michael Duffy closed his homily at that service with, "We come to bury Myke Judge's body, but not his spirit. We come to bury his hands, but not his good works. We come to bury his heart, but not his love. Never his love."[2]

[1]Michael Daly, *Daily News* (New York), February 11, 2002.

Shannon Stapleton, September 11, 2001, Photojournalist.

[2]Stephen Todd, *Daily Ponderables*, September 11, 2017.

"Slain Priest: 'Bury His Heart, But Not His Love.'" September 8, 2011, *NPR* morning edition.

Crafton: Living with Limitations

"Just because you're disabled doesn't mean you're not anything else. Have you lost an ability you used to have? Something you loved? Have you had to say good-bye to it? Maybe there's another way or another place in which you can still do it, or something like it."— Barbara Crafton, *eMo* from The Geranium Farm (geraniumfarm.org), August 16, 2018.

The Center for Disease Control (CDC) has reported on its website that 61 million adults, or about one fourth of adults in this country, have a disability that majorly impacts their lives. The most common disability involves mobility, affecting one in seven adults. This limitation is more common in women, especially those in the South who are of lower income. The most common disability in younger adults is cognitive impairment.

Barbara Crafton, who recently visited St. Mark's Episcopal Church, Little Rock, writes an almost daily email *eMo* from the "Geranium Farm," including a picture of artwork related to her story. One week she featured a Van Gogh painting, "Summer Wheat Field with Cypresses," painted in the artist's last year, a view from a window in his room at a mental facility.

My experience is that each of us has what the Apostle Paul calls a "thorn" in our flesh. If we think another person doesn't suffer from this, we are very mistaken.

We have a choice of how to respond to a disability. More and more I believe we can ask in our prayers *how that thorn brings fresh light into our lives*. Those in recovery will say that their addiction brought them to an alternative life they never dreamed of. I see people with cancer changing and bettering the lives of others until the very end. I see parents with handicapped children who are experts in patience and kindness and love.

There is a new pathway. It may not mean overcoming the disability, but rather waking up to a divine message, or being opened up to a new direction in becoming the person God has created us to be.

September 29 Angels

"For he will command his angels concerning you to guard you in all your ways."—Psalm 91:11.

September 29: The Feast of St. Michael and All Angels

Today, the next to the last day of September, is the Feast Day of St. Michael and All Angels. Above my desk in my home office, a carved stone hanging by my window bears a painted picture of St. Michael with his sword. Michael is almost the first thing I see when I lift my eyes from my computer. St. Michael lives in stained glass, overcoming evil just outside my church's chapel. I give thanks for St. Michaels in my life—and for angels who have been by my side in troublesome times, lending me courage to go on.

I think of some of our favorite fictional angels. There is Angel Second Class Clarence Odbody, played by Henry Travers in the timeless Frank Capra Christmas movie, *It's a Wonderful Life* (1946). Clarence saves George Bailey, played by Jimmy Stewart, from bankruptcy and suicide.

Whenever I hear a bell ring, I wonder if an angel has just earned his wings!

Then there is my all-time favorite movie angel, the suave angel named Dudley, played to the essence by Cary Grant in the Samuel Goldwyn Christmas classic, *The Bishop's Wife* (1947). Dudley comes to save the life and marriage of Bishop Henry Brougham, played by David Niven. Loretta Young plays his wife Julia.

Whenever I visit my Bishop's office, I always look around to see where Dudley is.

As I talk to people in spiritual direction, I listen to hear if they speak about "angels" in their lives—people whom they encounter over time, or who stand by them or lead them through tough situations or around impossible obstacles. Angels are life changing and life-giving. They are messengers, true tellers, who see God in us and, as the angel Gabriel did to Mary, proclaim that *God is in us*—when we never had a clue.

Give thanks for the angels in your life. Repay them by being a Dudley or Clarence or Michael—or another angel to someone else you meet.

Precious Present

"God speaks to every individual through what happens to them moment by moment. The events of each moment are stamped with the will of God ... we find all that is necessary in the present moment."

—Jean Pierre de Caussade in *Abandonment to Divine Providence* (1921).

We spoke earlier about Spencer Johnson's famous book about living in the present, *The Precious Present* (in *A Daily Spiritual Rx for Advent, Christmas, and Epiphany*). C. S. Lewis writes that God speaks to us in the present, not in the past or future. Many mindfulness exercises are about getting into the present moment, living in the present moment, as are many of our spiritual practices such as walking the labyrinth, using the rosary, waiting in silence, and walking meditation.

Anthony de Mello in his book *Sadhana* teaches us that living in our body and not living out of our head keeps us grounded. Our bodies keep us in the present moment grounded to the earth. Our mind is always in the future or the past. Spending time in nature connects us to the present. The trees photosynthesize, transform the energy within us to see beauty. Beauty grounds us in the present. Being and playing with children keeps us in the present, for that is where they live.

Spiritual Experience

"It may be possible to find explanations of spiritual experiences such as ours, but I have often tried to explain my own and have succeeded only in giving the story of it. I know the feeling it gave me and the results it has brought, but I realize I may never fully understand its deeper why and how."—Bill Wilson in *As Bill Sees It* (Alcoholics Anonymous, 1967), p. 313.

Bill Wilson was not the only one to have a spiritual experience. I daily meet with people who gradually, reluctantly, and sometimes embarrassingly tell me stories about their spiritual experiences. We are still under the influence of the age of enlightenment and reason. We only know what we can explain.

We may fear sharing anything that comes from mystery. For many people, these spiritual experiences occur outside in nature. Suddenly we feel arms holding us up. We sense a presence beside us. Some have the experience in a house of worship. A flickering candle produces what looks like holy smoke. Some grow into awareness at the Eucharist. They leave the rail at peace with what is going on in their lives. Many people remember a religious experience at the birth of a child, or seeing a newborn for the first time.

Birds often can contribute to a transcendent experience. I remember the Sunday after the death of a dear friend, Jane Murray. I saw a wild goose fly close by the window of our church sanctuary. I had never seen that before and haven't seen it since. The wild goose is the Celtic symbol for the Holy Spirit.

Candles can often contribute to our enlightenment. I was recently meeting and talking with a friend who saw the reflected light of the burning candle beside us through a window, and the reflection made it appear to be on a tree outside our window. He spoke up, "I see a burning bush!" These are all "burning bush" experiences, and we should take our shoes off when we encounter them.

John McCain

"But the souls of the righteous are in the hand of God,

and no torment will ever touch them.

In the eyes of the foolish they seemed to have died,

and their departure was thought to be a disaster,

and their going from us to be their destruction;

but they are at peace.

For though in the sight of others they were punished,

their hope is full of immortality.

Having been disciplined a little, they will receive great good,

because God tested them and found them worthy of himself.

Those who trust in him will understand truth,

and the faithful will abide with him in love,

because grace and mercy are upon his holy ones,

and he watches over his elect."—Wisdom 3:1-5, 9.

Along with many Americans, I have spent several days watching memorials to Senator John McCain. On Saturday morning, I watched the service at the National Cathedral. I became awed at the Cathedral almost thirty years ago when our friends Joanne and Allan Meadors introduced us to it through the National Cathedral Association, and we became hooked. For twenty years we visited it at least twice a year, often staying at the College of Preachers on its grounds. I am still reeling from this memorable service on Saturday morning held in such a familiar sacred space.

Former Senator Kelly Ayotte read these beautiful scriptural words from the Book of Wisdom, which are recommended for the Burial Office.

What a tribute that a man can so inspire us through his death—by how he lived, and even how he planned his burial service. I can barely talk about it, much less write about it. Many of us were reduced to tears by Meghan McCain's tribute to her father. This is an actual sign of greatness, when a man so involved in politics is also deeply cared for and loved by his children.

The entire service was inspiring, a remembrance of an icon— of someone who made mistakes and owned up to them; who dared to cross the aisle at the Senate to listen to representatives of the other party; who learned to speak his own truth and face the consequences.

Many believe that he grew in character because of his five years of captivity in North Vietnam as a prisoner of war. Most of us cannot imagine what that was like. McCain is a role model for us of someone who turned his trials into gold.

I see many lives in captivity, not in the way McCain's was, but caught in the captivity of an addiction. I daily encounter ordinary men and women who have learned from and come out of that life into what Christians would call a life of resurrection, an alternative life beyond anything they could have dreamed. Many who knew them in the past can no longer recognize them—physically, mentally, or spiritually.

John McCain's service was a service of resurrection, a reminder for all of us that there is another way to live and that we can begin that journey before death.

How Do I Listen?

"How
Do I
Listen to others?
As if everyone were my Master
Speaking to me
His
Cherished
Last
Words."
—Hafiz, *The Gift* (renderings by Daniel James Ladinsky).

Listening skills are paramount with spiritual friends. I remember one person I met with for spiritual direction who talked for the entire hour. I never spoke a word. I kept waiting for her to take a breath, but it didn't seem to happen. At first, I couldn't understand why she came; but gradually I sensed that she just needed someone to listen to her, to acknowledge the God within her. This became more evident after she sent several other people to me for direction because she said I was so helpful! I also realized that she was a gift to me, teaching me how to listen.

There are many listening exercises we can practice enabling us to be experienced listeners. One is used by a grief recovery group, *Walking the Mourner's Path*. At the first meeting of those who are grieving the death of a loved one, the participants divide into pairs, and each person tells the other about his or her loved one. Then they all return to the group as each listener tells the group about the

243

person being grieved by his or her partner. Even though the pairs never work together again, a bond between them often develops that lasts for the eight weeks of the program and longer.

Buechner: A Good Steward of Pain

"I am sure there are one hundred and six ways we have of coping with pain. Another way is to be a good steward of it."—Frederick Buechner in *A Crazy Holy Grace* (Zondervan, 2017).

Two book clubs in which I am participating have read *A Crazy Holy Grace,* a recent collection of some of Frederick Buechner's essays about pain and memory. In one story from a previous book, *The Eyes of the Heart,* Buechner writes about a special series of rooms in his home that constitute his sacred space. He describes his writing space, the library—the largest room, with ceiling-high shelves of books, including the *Uncle Wiggly Series,* his first editions, and sermons of John Donne. Also in the room are unique objects meaningful to him: framed autographs of heroes such as Queen Elizabeth I and inscribed portraits of heroes such as Mark Twain and Anthony Trollope.

In his imagination, Buechner then invites people from his past into what he calls his Magic Kingdom. He carries on a loving and humorous conversation with his ninety-four-year-old grandmother Naya, whom he obviously dearly loves. As he tells it, she describes their relationship as "a marriage made in heaven. I loved to talk, and you loved to listen." Buechner asks her about death. Naya describes it as "stepping off of a streetcar before it has quite come to a stop."

Buechner has written extensively about his mother, who deals with her pain by burying it or forgetting about it; and his father, who deadens his pain with alcohol, and finally a tragic suicide when

Buechner is ten years old. Buechner seems to have worked through difficulties in those relationships by writing about them. However, he still cannot invite his parents into his sacred space because of their fears that they may be too much or too little.

Buechner models for us two ways to let God enable us to work through our pain from the past. First, we can return in our imagination to a sacred space to be with those with whom we feel safe, and let them guide us through our pain. Second, when we are not comfortable dialoguing directly with those with whom we had difficulty, we can dialogue with them on paper. He believes that God works to heal us through both methods.

Jean Shinoda Bolen: Soul Work

"You have the need and the right to spend part of your life caring for your soul. It is not easy. You have to resist the demands of the work-oriented, often defensive, element in your psyche that measures life only in terms of output—how much you produce—not in terms of the quality of your life experiences. To be a soulful person means to go against all the pervasive, prove-yourself values of our culture and instead treasure what is unique and internal and valuable in yourself and your own personal evolution."—Jean Shinoda Bolen.

We can learn so much about ourselves and our souls from Jean Shinoda Bolen. Her book, *Goddesses in Everywoman,* teaches us about the Artemis, the Athena, the Hestia, the Hera, the Demeter, the Persephone, and the Aphrodite in our own psyches, and how each relates to and cares for our soul both positively and negatively.

Bolen's writings bring us so much wisdom for this journey. She empowers us during troublesome situations to stay the heroine, knowing and believing that answers will come and that things will change. She warns against regressing into embodying the victim—a scenario in which all our energy is used defensively, because we view the situation as caused by others. When we identify ourselves as the victim, our soul cannot breathe.

I love the story of Psyche's journey to reunite with her husband, Eros, the masculine part of her personality. One of her onerous tasks is to sort a large number of different seeds. The sorting is done by an out-of-the-box, unusual group of insects or ants that appear to solve her dilemma. These ants may represent our intuitive function, something beyond cognitive ability that represents a potential inside of us. In confusing situations, this natural intuition will come to our aid if we can stay grounded as the heroine.

Other tasks that enable women to connect to their masculine side involve allowing the feminine to gain power but remain compassionate; learning to see the big picture; developing the ability to say no. These stories of tough situations where we have the opportunity to learn about ourselves are some of the many ways we can nurture our soul. We let it take deep breaths so we can wake up from a deep sleep. This is soul work.

Labyrinths: Looking Forward and Expectations

"Not too long ago I walked a labyrinth for the first time in my life. I had flirted with labyrinths for years, but my expectations were so high that I kept finding reasons not to walk one. I did not want to hurry. I did not want to share the labyrinth with anyone who might distract me. I did not want to be disappointed. I looked forward to walking a labyrinth so much that looking forward to it kept me from doing it for years."—Barbara Brown Taylor in *An Altar in the World* (HarperCollins, 2006).

With her usual honesty, Barbara Brown Taylor reminds us of how our expectations of a spiritual practice can keep us from the practice. We may have fears that we will not find in a spiritual practice the fulfillment that so many of our friends speak of. The reality is that it is impossible for us to be proficient in *all* the spiritual practices. We can try them out, give each one some time, and afterwards may realize that one or more of them are not our best way to connect to God.

God has provided a smorgasbord of ways for us to connect to the holy. Some practices may be helpful at one stage in our life and not in another. At one time in my life, Morning Prayer and *Lectio Divina* stabilized my body and soul. At other times, a daily walk around my neighborhood centered me before I went to work at the hospital. Now my central practice is writing; it has become my best form of prayer.

I talk to spiritual friends about not giving up or never considering a spiritual practice again. Listen to the Spirit within. My experience is that we will often receive a nudge to return to a practice we tried previously when we are now in a different stage of life. What a blessing that we have so many ways to connect to God.

I struggle with Centering Prayer. I have difficulty just sitting still and calming the committee in my head; but I do not give up. However, walking the labyrinth is a natural for me. Concentrating on following its turns gives my mind a much-needed rest. Walking a path allows me to live in the *present* again rather than in the past or future. My surrender to the winding of the labyrinth—a metaphor for our spiritual journey—is a reminder of how we stay connected to God without and within. Journeying with others on the path also enables us also to see God in our neighbor.

Early in walking the labyrinth, we come very close to the center. "Aha, I have arrived;" but immediately after that premature thought, I am suddenly back around the edge. I find myself close to the edge near the end and think I still have a long way to go. Not long after comes the realization that I am finished!

I need a meditation with movement to connect my soul to God. The labyrinth, dance, yoga, praying in color, the rosary, and other bodily movement meditations are ways to achieve quietness for those of us overwhelmed by the busyness of life. They allow us to "park" our minds, so we are not constantly thinking about the past or the future.

My experience is that I do not always receive the gift of connection when I reach the labyrinth center. Instead, this sense of presence may come to me anywhere along the path. I remember one New Year's Eve when I walked the labyrinth at Christ Church. It was chilly, and I wore a shawl with fringes that looked like a drape that might cover your grandmother's piano. Halfway out, an unusual warmth enveloped me. I felt the love of my grandmothers surrounding me like the comfort of the long black shawl.

Often as I walk, I meditate on the words of Thich Nhat Hanh[1], a Vietnamese spiritual guide known for his walking meditations: "People say that walking on water is a miracle, but to me walking on earth is a real miracle."

1Thich Nhat Hanh, *The Long Road Turns to Joy: A Guide to Walking Meditation* (Parallax Press, 2007).

A Prayer of St. Chrysostom

"Almighty God, you have given us grace at this time with one accord to make our common supplication to you; and you have promised through your well-beloved Son that when two or three are gathered together in his Name you will be in the midst of them: Fulfill now, O Lord, our desires and petitions as may be best for us; granting us in this world knowledge of your truth, and in the age to come life everlasting. *Amen.*" —*The Book of Common Prayer* (Church Publishing, Inc.), p. 102.

How often I have said this prayer at the end of the daily Morning Prayer Office from *The Book of Common Prayer* and shared with others desperately seeking hope. When we pray together, we affirm that God hears our prayer, even before we pray. As I say this prayer, I remember that C. S. Lewis always reminds us that we pray not to change God but to change ourselves.

As we pray this prayer in the Daily Office of Morning Prayer, we also can feel connected to all others in all places praying Morning Prayer along with us. That is why I have often joined a group of pray-ers saying prayers at a certain hour of the day for a specific person we know is in need or distress. The deep realization that others are praying petitions for the same person or cause all over the country or the world is a force of nature. Sometimes we may later find out whether that person is safe or has improved; but always, always, we are changed.

St. Chrysostom's prayer also reminds us of how fleeting fame is. Chrysostom, an archbishop of Constantinople in the late 4th century, often referred to as the "golden mouthed" because of his excellence in preaching, was the most famous early Christian preacher and most prolific writer, exceeded only by Augustine. He was outspoken about abuses in the Church and politics. His legacy is still a dominant influence in the Eastern Orthodox tradition, and we celebrate his feast day on September 13. However, I know only a few preachers in our Church who quote his famous Easter sermon, most often at the Vigil.

This daily prayer constitutes all that most of us in the Western Church still possess to remember him by; but because of its power and wisdom, it is more than enough.

Beautiful People

"The most beautiful people we have known are those who have known defeat, known suffering, known struggle, known loss, and have found their way out of the depths. These persons have an appreciation, a sensitivity, and an understanding of life that fills them with compassion, gentleness, and a deep loving concern. Beautiful people do not just happen."—Elizabeth Kübler-Ross in *Death: The Final Stage of Growth* (Simon & Schuster, 1986), p. 96.

I met at least two beautiful people today. I went to say prayers and give ashes to an older member of our congregation in the hospital, as it is Ash Wednesday. As I was waiting at the elevator with my silver pix filled with a small amount of ashes, an African American wheelchair attendant asked me about the black ash on my forehead. I reminded him it was Ash Wednesday. He asked for ashes, as it was his Church's tradition as well. He commented that he usually takes another elevator, but today he stepped into this one, and now he knew why.

So we had "ashes to go" right there as we waited for the elevators to come down. Here was a gentle, sensitive man looking for God's presence in all he does, especially in busy times. I do not know any of his life circumstances. We gave each other a blessing, and after the elevator came down, we parted as I went up to Michael's floor.

Michael was sitting up, and his stepdaughter was sitting by him. I will always remember his amazing smile as he saw me and reached out to greet me with his left arm tethered to intravenous tubing. Both bandaged legs were elevated in his wheelchair. He had fallen and broken his hip, but he talked about having a puncture in his heel. Kindness and love shone out through his dementia as he apologized for not standing up when I entered his room.

His stepdaughter described him as the sweetest man she had ever known; and just in these few minutes I knew it was true. I longed to stay for hours and simply listen to him talk, even though his confused conversation about his children and his life made no sense. I craved being in the presence of someone who seemed to know only love and kindness, even though he was not connected to mundane reality. I hope I can share Michael with those I talk with about spiritual direction and remind spiritual friends that *love* and *God* need not be rational understandings. Love has a distinctive "aura" that can fill a room fuller and faster than the most beautiful or intelligent phrases, something like poetry.

There are many books about dementia and Alzheimer's. Spiritual friends often ask about finding love and God as they watch a loved one slip away in dementia. Not all are like Michael.

I usually share two books that have been helpful. Susan Cushman has written *Tangles and Plaques: A Mother and Daughter Face Alzheimer's,* about a harder situation; and Frank Broyles has published a very practical book about caring for his wife, who has Alzheimer's: *Coach Broyles' Playbook for Alzheimer's Caregivers: A Practical Tip Guide.* I think some of the most beautiful people that Kübler-Ross talks about are not only the dying, but those with dementia and those who care for them.

Charleston: Trees

"My great grandfather told me this long ago and I never forgot it: trees are the keepers of secrets. The Creator gave them this honor because they are infinitely patient and trustworthy. So if you have a burden on your heart, something that has bothered you for a long time, something you wish you could finally let go, then take it to the tree. You will know the right one when you see it. It will be an old tree with many branches. Go stand beneath it and tell your story. Then when you walk away what you have said will stay there, in the safe-keeping of the old tree, and you will be burdened by it no more."
—Bishop Steven Charleston, Daily Facebook Page (9/1/2018.)

My grandfather and my father both introduced me to the spirituality of trees. My grandfather took me on nature walks on his farm each week, along the Mattaponi River and its marshlands. My father was a forester who planted millions of trees. I still grieve to see trees cut down. I often like to imagine what secrets old trees have, as I briefly touch them, passing by them on my way to appointments.

All of our children spend much more time outdoors than I do. I don't remember teaching them the value of this. Maybe this wisdom was passed down by my grandfather, whom they never knew, and my father, whom they barely knew. This may not be true, but I will still treasure this possibility in my imagination.

I believe that we meet God in the outdoors so much easier than in most indoor places. Sitting and standing by trees reduces the tension in our bodies. Our minds slow down to a slightly lower speed. We become grounded to the earth. We begin to live in the present moment, and we meet the God of our understanding in that moment.

When we are at peace, we do not obsess about the past. We may remember our mistakes, but we have the desire to move on, seeking to learn from them. We surrender to the experience, and for a few seconds stop worrying about the future. For a brief moment, we become the person God created us to be.

We know from biology class that trees save our lives by changing our carbon dioxide waste into life-giving oxygen that enables us to breathe again. Trees also save our lives mentally and spiritually by standing as a constant reminder of a God who has provided for us beauty beyond our imagination.

Outside my window is a canopy of trees that have become like old friends. The sun is almost up. I will wait until sunrise and look out so I can see them in all their glory before beginning this day. I give thanks for all who have led me outdoors to the trees. Perhaps I can do the same today for someone else.

Buechner: Parents

"'Honor your Father and your mother,' says the Fifth Commandment (Exodus 20:12). Honor them for having taken care of you before you were old enough to take care of yourself."
—Frederick Buechner.

Buechner reminds us of the Fifth Commandment: to honor our parents. He explains that we are to honor them because they loved us and cared for us.

I sat with a group of friends last week and we all spontaneously started talking about scars we received from our parents, particularly our mothers. Some were abused or neglected by parents. Some did not receive the love they had hoped for from their parents. Some had parents who never grew up to be the adults and mentors that a child needed for protection. Buechner reminds us that our parents also had scars. They were doing the best they could with what they knew. Buechner also reminds us that we should always be grateful to them for giving us the gift of life.

Our experience also was that there were always adults in our lives who could be mentors for us when our parents were not able to do so. Some of the group were actually doing this now for other children or adults.

We then wondered what our children would say about us—thinking of the scars we may have given them, because of our own imperfections. Our prayers become that we can still make living amends for the harm we have done; and that we will be able to reverse some of the behavior we have inherited, while also honoring the richness of our heritage.

Spiritual Practices and Social Action

"Spiritual practices undergird social action. Accordingly, socially active congregations must make spiritual practices essential to their mission. There is no division between prayer and protest, between spirituality and social concern. Contemplation deepens our spirits and broadens our sensitivities. Action expands the scope of our spiritual sensitivity. And God can enlarge our hearts to see God's presence in every human and all creation, and to respond with grace and compassion."—Bruce G. Epperly, "What Does It Mean to Have a Savior?" in *The Christian Century* (9/16/2018).

The Christian life is richer if we can maintain spiritual disciplines and social activism at the same time, so we achieve a kind of balance. One practice leads to the other and nourishes and affirms the other. Through both ways, we learn about the Christ in ourselves and the Christ in each other.

Many who support social justice do not seem to connect to or affirm a supporting spirituality. Consequently, social issues sometimes consume them, and we can detect no visible presence of love in their actions. There also are those with deep spirituality but no sense of social justice. Often their spirituality turns so inward that it becomes stagnant and cannot grow. I have also had other experiences suggesting the relationship between the two is not so simple.

My story unfolds with the death of someone I loved. This drew me back to the spiritual life of which I had a taste in my youth. For years I simply learned and read and prayed and practiced spiritual disciplines daily. I was one of those "groupies" who went to every possible conference and retreat I could find. I never spoke out or participated in any social justice action. I blamed my inaction on being an introvert. Eventually, my heart could no longer contain the injustices to women, African Americans, immigrants, and gays. I had to speak out, sometimes boldly, often quietly—more often writing about this discrimination.

My "spiritual" excuse for the delay is biblical, of course. After Paul's conversion, and before he started his ministry, this is his story: "I did not confer with any human being nor did I go up to Jerusalem to those who were already apostles before, but I went away at once into Arabia, and afterwards I returned to Damascus. Then after three years I did go up to Jerusalem to visit Cephas and stayed with him for fifteen days" (Galatians 1:16-18). Paul then goes on to say he went to Syria and Cilicia and was unknown to the churches of Judea; but after fourteen years he finally went up to Jerusalem with Barnabas.

My time in "Arabia" was much longer. It took me twenty years of spiritual reflection before I began to make a dent in any social action. And it was almost twenty more years before I let my feet do the talking and took part in two women's marches. Now I make calls, write letters, and financially help social justice causes and the candidates who support them. I hope that my spiritual practices keep me centered on the God who loves us all, and that being a voice of protest toward social injustices leads me to the people in whom the God of my understanding abides.

Music

"After silence, that which comes nearest to expressing the inexpressible is music."—Aldous Huxley.

When my husband and I were in training at the University of Iowa, the Department of Otolaryngology (Ear, Nose, and Throat) put on a program in which the entertainment was a slide show of scenes from Iowa called "Iowa: A Place to Grow." The background music was the first movement of Beethoven's Sixth Symphony, or the Pastoral Symphony. It is playing now on our Public Radio station. Every time I hear it, I think of our four years in Iowa City.

It is amazing how, over the years, we remember only the pleasurable parts; and so, as Beethoven's Sixth plays, the delightful memories are exactly what flash through my mind: the friends we studied with, my first job as a pediatric radiologist and the amazing colleagues who taught me how to be a pediatrician and a radiologist; taking trips on Sunday afternoons with our two boys to small towns, looking for antiques. One of our favorite towns was West Branch, the birthplace of Herbert Hoover.

I remember the first house we were able to buy with the help of my husband's parents; the fresh food from Iowa farms; Sunday dinners at the University of Iowa; concerts at Hancher Auditorium; the city park just around the corner from our house on Park Road; the enormous elm tree in our backyard and the apple tree between our garage and the house; riding our bicycle for two with our two boys on it unprotected; visiting the Amana Colonies; weekends in Davenport on the Mississippi River; and brief trips to Chicago.

I hear the music, and I am immediately back in Iowa with old friends. Music transports us to new places, but perhaps more poignantly, takes us to places we *have* been. These are soul trips that bring us comfort and peace, if we will take the time to allow them back into our minds.

Music can be one of our best travel agents to times and places where we were loved and cared for. This can lead us to a place of gratitude for opportunities, friends, and teachers, and many whom we forgot to thank at the time. But let's both take time to do so this day.

Cloud of Witnesses at the Eucharist

"The gifts of God for the people of God."—Holy Eucharist II, *The Book of Common Prayer* (Church Publishing, 1979), p. 264.

I keep thinking and praying for two women in my spiritual direction class, Vicki and Diane, who live on the North and South Carolina coasts whose towns are being battered by this storm. My mind wanders back to Kanuga Conference Center at one graduation at the Haden Institute for Spiritual Direction. We are in the Chapel of Transfiguration. A flute is playing in the background. The eight women who are graduating process in and sit in chairs in front of the raised altar. They share their stories and their journey and the work they have done while learning how to lead others to find God in their lives. They receive their certificates and plaques, and then we prepare for taking the Eucharist together around the altar above us.

"The gifts of God for the people of God." As the bread and wine are offered, they ask each person to come up the several steps to the altar to give herself the bread and wine.

Suddenly I panic. There is no rail for the steps to this altar, as there is at St. Luke's and at St. Mark's. Kind members built the rails after I came as a deacon and realized I had difficulty with steps. I say a prayer of gratitude for the kindhearted and thoughtful people of both congregations. What will I do tonight?

I remember the ten amazing women that I had spent the past year with studying spiritual direction. We have prayed together, eaten together, done spiritual direction, verbatims, and dream work, and most especially shared our life together.

Suddenly my group surrounds me. They do not miss a beat. "We will all go to Communion together, not separately," they whisper. They will all stand with me at the bottom of the stairs to the altar. Ann, the priest in our group, will offer bread, and Bridget will serve wine.

There are not words to describe what it was like standing in the middle of that long, feminine line with my spiritual friends at the foot of the altar that seemed so far away—but instead was moved to be right in front of us. I had a glimpse of what it is like to feel Christ not only inside of me, but beside me, standing, walking with me on this journey. I felt myself surrounded by a cloud of witnesses.

I wish I could share a picture today from the following year at our own class' graduation. I hold that group of spiritual friends in my prayers daily, and now especially Vicki on the coast of North Carolina and Diane in South Carolina as they often endure storms near their homes. I will never forget their kindness. I have experienced how well they care for others. I pray fervently that someone is caring for them today.

Natural Disasters

"When evening came, his disciples went down to the sea, got into a boat, and started across the sea to Capernaum. It was not dark, and Jesus had not yet come to them. The sea became rough because a strong wind was blowing. When they had rowed about three or four miles, they saw Jesus walking on the sea and coming near the boat, and they were terrified. But he said to them, 'It is I; do not be afraid.' Then they wanted to take him into the boat, and immediately the boat reached the land toward which they were going."—John 6:16-21.

Fifteen years ago, on September 16, Hurricane Ivan made a direct hit on the town of Orange Beach along the Alabama Gulf Coast near the Florida line. There were twenty-five deaths in the United States, including fourteen in Florida. This category-three storm caused major destruction to an area that had become our family's beloved vacation spot for years.

My heart goes out to the people on the North Carolina and South Carolina coasts who later were visited by Hurricane Florence. I remember the days of looking at any picture that might show if the storm had destroyed our special place. It was weeks before we could return to our condo on the fourth floor and go inside to survey the damage.

We hardly recognized the building. Vast parts of the front facade were gone. Wind and water had destroyed every condo on the first floor. Two large glass doors had blown out of the condo, and furniture was blown out of the gapping, exposed spaces. The

266

elevators were not functioning; so it was a major trek up and down the stairs once we figured out where they were. We made multiple trips to dispose of the rotting food left in the refrigerator.

My clearest memory is of the disorientation we experienced when so many of the familiar markers were gone. Besides the damage to the front of our condominium, street signs were no longer there, familiar buildings had disappeared, and parts of the roads were destroyed. We had to take detours through even more unfamiliar places.

Such a natural disaster is a reminder of what happens when we face major emotional crises or significant changes in our personal lives—such as the death of a loved one, a life-threatening illness, a divorce, a move, or even a new job. At such times, all of our usual markers can disappear. We may become disoriented. Decisions can become agonizingly difficult to make. It is sometimes hard to find our way. Often it is as though we are in a foreign country, and the people surrounding us are speaking a language we have never heard before.

It is important to recognize this state of mind, to take care of ourselves, and to be open to receiving help. If we try to white-knuckle it and get through the crisis alone, the burden often becomes intolerable. My experience is that *recovery comes* and normalcy returns with the blessed support and help of friends and community.

The Art of Pilgrimage

"We shall not cease from exploration

And the end of all our exploring

Will be to arrive where we started

And know the place for the first time."—T. S. Eliot, *Little Gidding*.

I repeatedly return to Phil Cousineau's book *The Art of Pilgrimage: The Seeker's Guide to Making Travel Sacred* whenever I am preparing for a trip and hoping to make the journey a pilgrimage.

Cousineau's family traveled often in his childhood. He relates how his father thought travel was good for the mind, while his mother felt it was good for the soul. Cousineau reminds us that a *traveler* visits a place. A *pilgrim* allows a place to become a part of one's inner self. As travelers we often plan trips, and then, upon getting to our destination, experience a sense of unfulfilled expectation. This disappointment results from the way we engage with the place, not because of the shortcomings in the site itself.

The Celts would tell us to imagine the moment of our departure as the crossing of a threshold of a door.

Cousineau also asks us to imagine our first memorable journey. What images rise up in our soul? They may be a childhood trip to the family gravesite; a visit to relatives who live on a farm; or an outing to a religious site accompanied by our favorite aunt.

Do these feelings have any connection with our lives today? The author asks us if there are places sacred to us and/or our family that we long to visit? He suggests that as we uncover what we long for, we will discover *who we are*.

Cousineau reminds us we will reconnect to our soul, the part of God within us, by learning to be *aware* and to *listen* to our surroundings. On a pilgrimage we are to look—not overlook; and to listen intently to everything around us. We can practice listening to music in solitude to get back into the habit of listening to our surroundings. Keeping a journal may help us look more closely as we seek to describe what we are seeing.

There is an old Nigerian saying that "the day on which one starts out is not the time to start one's preparation." We are to begin the Sacred Journey with our journal. He encourages us to keep sacred a silent "alone" part of our day to write in our journal. Our journal can help us relive our pilgrimage; but we can also make it possible to relive the journey by bringing back pictures, stones, or shells, as Anne Morrow Lindbergh writes about in *Gift from the Sea*.

We are also to plan ahead how we will re-energize ourselves each day. It is important to be open to serendipity, coincidences, and even distractions that may take us off our planned path. I remember a time I spent at the College of Preachers at the National Cathedral. I was walking through the Cathedral near the entrance when a sizeable group of elementary students of around ten years old hurried in. They were distracting my silent mediation. But then I most vividly remember one young boy tilting back his head and looking up at the high-vaulted ceilings and immediately shouting out, "Wow!!" To this day, I can still see and hear that young prophet.

Holy Places and Holy Stories

"Bethlehem and Nazareth and Jerusalem remind us that it is to possible to touch, and hold and see God, even in this life, in the guise of helpless infants, worried parents, broken bodies and empty tombs."—Br. James Koester, SSJE, from "Brother, Give Us a Word," a daily email sent to friends and followers of the Society of Saint John the Evangelist (SSJE.org).

Many of you have visited the Holy Land and been to these "thin places." For me, visiting these shrines has made the stories of what happened at each place more vivid. For those who have not traveled to these sites, the stories are still powerful and often can come alive in our own imagination or through art. There are also places that *represent* these holy shrines that can bring them alive. I am thinking of the National Cathedral's Bethlehem Chapel, Children's Chapel, Chapel of Joseph of Arimathea, and Chapel of the Resurrection.

Each holy site can also represent a part of our own lives.

Our Bethlehem is not only the location of our birth, but the place where we begin to feel alive, reborn—that we are becoming the person God created us to be. Our "Bethlehem" often is a retreat refuge where our life was changed. Our "Nazareth" can be not only the place where we were raised, but also the places where we are still cared for, nourished, and restored. For many, their Nazareth is their church or spiritual community.

Jerusalem is the holiest of places. It is the place where God most clearly lives. It is where we suffer, and also where parts of us have to die. But miraculously, out of this suffering, we find resurrection. I am mindful of Jerusalem most often in a grief recovery group called Walking the Mourner's Path. It is with the participants we see great suffering transformed into new life. The work involves honoring loved ones who have died and becoming wounded healers to others who have suffered.

Each city images a new life, a new birth, a resurrection. Renewal can be messier at some places and easier and gentler at others.

Today may we contemplate where these holy cities reside in our lives. Where are the places we go to be reborn, to be nourished, and to be resurrected out of suffering?

Buechner: Prayer

"WE ALL PRAY whether we think of it as praying or not."—Frederick Buechner.

Frederick Buechner reminds us that the sigh that automatically leaps from us when we see beauty, art, music, mouth-watering comfort food, or old friends can be identified as the *thanks, wow* prayers that Anne Lamott has written about in *Help, Thanks, Wow: The Three Essential Prayers* (Riverhead, 2012). There is something inside of us, the God in us, the Christ in us, the Spirit within us, that cannot help but direct us back to the connection we came from. This is another word for prayer: a connection to the place from which we came.

Buechner also reminds us of all the stories in the New Testament about how God assures us that persistence in prayer can make a difference in our lives. The *Hound of Heaven* is in pursuit of us, and we are to follow that example. If nothing else, we are also heeding C. S. Lewis' advice to "act as if" we believe in that power greater than ourselves—and eventually something happens. The 12-step groups put it more simply, "fake it, till you make it."

Buechner also suggests that even if we consider prayer to be merely talking to ourselves, it is not a bad practice. It's similar to the Ignatian *examen,* in which we consider what is happening in our life. We review our day and discover insights that we might never have known if we had not stopped to consider *where we need help* and *which path might be best.* We soon learn that we are called to the road less traveled—which leads to many more prayers.

Rule of Life

"The Rule of Benedict is concerned with life: what it's about, what it demands, how to love it. And it has not failed a single generation."—Joan Chittister in *The Rule of Benedict: A Spirituality for the 21st Century* (Crossroad, 2010), p. 2.

Brother Michael Gallagher, OSB, spoke at this weekend's Community of Hope Retreat about evaluating our Benedictine Rule of Life. He asked us to consider what was the *good news* our religion talks about. His belief is that the *good news* is that we are one with God. We have been loved into life by God. God calls us constantly to maintain that connection. How do *we* maintain it?

Michael then asked us to carry with us a pad on which to write down for one week everything we did hourly. That sounded like a daunting task. At the very least, we would get some ideas of where we were spending our energy; how well and when we were eating; how often we listened to the news; how much time we were spending with family; and how much work we were required to do at home. This assignment reminded me of looking at our checkbook or credit card report to see where we are spending our energy and our money.

Next he recommended we put on our calendar for each day, a time for morning prayers. The time spent and the type of prayer were not as important as doing it at the same time each day. Then he asked us to schedule a time for evening prayers—again, the same time each day. Lastly, he wanted us to write in a regular time at which to eat our meals each day. I am beginning to get his message. God calls us to faithfulness. If we attempt to invite God to be a part of a regular rhythm in our lives, we will find that God connection.

Michael promises us we do not have to worry as much about *what we do* in between the meals and prayers. God fills in the blanks: we will be led, especially through the interruptions in our lives. Michael made one suggestion regarding prayer, and that was that we include prayers of gratitude. My experience is that gratitude is the holy stickiness that can hold our life together. Well, now we are called to more adventure, a fresh look at our rule of life. More will be revealed.

Forgiveness/Healing

"But they could not find a way to take him in because of so many people. They made a hole in the roof over where Jesus stood. Then they let the bed with the sick man on it down before Jesus. When Jesus saw their faith, he said to the man, 'Friend, your sins are forgiven.'"—Luke 5:19-20.

Many of the healing stories of Jesus describe him first forgiving the sins of those who are afflicted, and then healing their physical ills. He sees a person's spiritual condition as a higher priority than any physical malady. He knows that he can bring more comfort by leading us to give up our resentments and abuses—before he tackles the physical pain. This has been my experience.

Awareness of the spiritual harms I have afflicted on others has brought me more pain than any physical illness. The pain I have caused my partners at work, my spouse, my children, my friends has been more overwhelming than the physical pain of broken bones or diseased organs. I have attempted to ease that spiritual pain with many remedies: food, alcohol, work, or busyness so that I do not have time to dwell on the wrongs I have done. Or perhaps I engage in exemplary works in some other area, hoping that will make up for the harm I perpetuated in other parts of my life.

The people coming to Jesus do not ask him for forgiveness of their sins. They ask for physical healing. They are deaf or blind to the spiritual ills that are blocking them. The good news is that Jesus knows where our pain is greatest, even when we do not realize it; and he lets us know that we are forgiven even before we ask!

This does not mean that we need not ask for forgiveness. My experience is that until we are aware of our sins and ask for forgiveness, we live with a terrible emotional pain. Sometimes we do not know where this pain is coming from, we just know it is there.

This story also can remind us that often it is our friends who bring us to Jesus for healing and forgiveness when we are "crippled," or out of answers, because the "pain relievers" are no longer working.

Awareness comes with prayer, spiritual exercises, spiritual direction, dreams. The good news is that once we have some awareness, the Gospel tells us we will be forgiven even before we ask! It is like going to your supervisor to ask for a raise and knowing before you get there that you will receive it!

Reading the Bible

"We don't go brain dead when we read the Scriptures. We need not hesitate to use our intellects—informed by many disciplines—as we approach the Scriptures. How does what you are reading in the Scriptures ring true to your own life experience and, if not, then what? The Anglican approach is to be on good speaking terms with Scripture, tradition, reason, and experience."—Br. Curtis Almquist, SSJE, from "Brother, Give Us a Word," a daily email sent to friends and followers of the Society of Saint John the Evangelist (SSJE.org).

The Bible is a library of many books. It is our road map, but not the final destination. It contains many writings of people seeking connection to God. We have so much to learn from them. We relate to their struggle, their joy, their sorrow, and the peace they find through a deep connection to God.

We are continually amazed how a passage can mean something different to us when we read it a week or a year or more later. This experience happens when we relate our lives, the lives of those around us, the world around us to what we are reading in Scripture.

Br. Almquist asks us to use our intellect, to think about what we are reading in Scripture. What was going on in the lives of the people when these books were written? Were they being persecuted? How different are our lives from theirs today?

Find out what other sources say. Br. Almquist is asking us to use our reason and experience. How does our own history enable us to understand what we are reading? We also have a rich tradition of holy mothers and fathers before us who have struggled and inwardly digested Holy Scripture. We are to investigate what they have to say.

I have always believed that the Holy Spirit did not stop working after the many books of the Bible were written. The Holy Spirit works in us and in those with whom we live in community, helping us to read and hear Scripture, and to discern what it is saying today in the twenty-first century.

My tradition encourages us to read each day from the Hebrew Bible, in addition to one of the Psalms, one of the letters of the New Testament, and one of the Gospel passages.

Here is my confession: I try to follow this rule. Sometimes I skip parts. Sometimes I read only the first and last verses of the Psalm and use them as a mantra for the day. Other times I choose only one reading, especially if it is a continuing story from the Hebrew Bible.

I love biblical narratives such as the story of Queen Esther, even if God is never mentioned in that book. I also try to follow the adventures of Paul and the early Christians—again, more stories. Some have become old friends, as in a recent reading about Paul meeting Aquila and Priscilla in Corinth after they had fled Rome. I do what I can. I have stopped beating myself up about not reading it all. I am learning that the Holy Spirit will speak to me in whatever measure I can receive. My job is to be faithful to the connection, sometimes very faithful, unfortunately, sometimes less faithful.

Vespers

"It is bad enough to cope with illness or worry during the day, but at night the hurts just seem to intensify as the darkness grows. Which is why I am inviting everyone to join me in the practice of vespers. Monks and nuns from many traditions keep regular hours of prayer. They sanctify day and night. Vespers is an evening prayer, a time to make the darkening hours holy. As night comes, let us pray for all those who will need help getting through it. Let our vesper prayer be a light for them to see."—Bishop Steven Charleston, Daily Facebook Page (9/25/2018).

Serendipity can become a sign for us to listen more intently about what is going on in our lives. Recently I received a call to keep Evening Prayer from many voices. They are getting my attention. Morning Prayer has been more of a routine most of my life; but I rarely remember to say evening prayers until I am almost asleep, and they may consist of a brief review of the day with a few sprinkles of gratitude thrown in for good measure.

The rector of our church, Danny Schieffler, asked our new Daughters of the King chapter to be more present at Evening Prayer on weekdays at our church. Our Community of Hope Retreat leader, Brother Michael Gallagher, OSB, almost the next day reminded us to keep regular evening prayers as well as morning prayers. Our church hosted a program by Tom Elliott on the spiritual exercises of St. Ignatius. The next day he talked about the evening *examen,* and how important it is in following this tradition. This morning we hear from Bishop Steven Charleston about nighttime prayers for all who need to be reminded of the presence and love of God when the world becomes dark.

My favorite evening prayers before bedtime are in the Order of Compline {*The Book of Common Prayer (BCP)* p. 127}. Many years ago, friends came to our house, or we went to theirs, to say this brief service together. How did we fit that time into our day? Were we less busy then, or more intentional?

My experience is that night can be more frightening for those who are alone and those in any kind of pain. The stimuli of the day, that keep us living our lives outwardly, lessen as darkness silently creeps in. At evening we feel the pull of the less familiar inward life. We do not know our paths on the inner life well and can be frightened; but by saying night prayers with others regularly, we can remind ourselves of Love's continued presence with us and within us.

"Keep watch, dear Lord, with those who work, or watch, or weep this night, and give your angels charge over those who sleep. Tend the sick, Lord Christ; give rest to the weary, bless the dying, soothe the suffering, pity the afflicted, shield the joyous; and all for your love's sake."—*BCP*, p. 134.

Sanford: Traveling Inward

"How quickly the days clatter by as we age, like a train rushing to some unknown station. Sit back and look to the vision within: the unexplored rooms of your heart, the open ground of your creativity, the hidden dimensions of your faith. Reflect on the reason for your travel and turn time to the will of your spirit. Sit back and look to the vision within, for when you go deeper, you go slower."—Bishop Steven Charleston Daily Facebook Page.

John Sanford's book, *The Kingdom Within: The Inner Meaning of Jesus' Sayings* (Lippincott Williams & Wilkins, 1970), is often one of the first helps recommended to people seeking to begin an inner journey. As his title suggests, Sanford affirms that the kingdom of God is really within us. Sanford, a Jungian analyst and Episcopal priest, was one of the first to apply depth psychology to Jesus' sayings, discussing personality types and the feminine and masculine aspects of personality. He also addresses the struggle between the spiritual and the physical, becoming aware of our own egocentricities and projections, the struggle to become conscious, and our identification with our outer mask, as each of these experiences relates to the teachings of Jesus.

Sanford talks extensively about the problem of evil and sin in the world, reminding us that Jesus himself had little to say about the sins of the flesh. He was more concerned about the deadlier sins of the spirit brought on by a lack of awareness that causes us to "miss the mark." Sanford reminds us that when we harbor in our hearts deep hatred toward our enemies, often we are projecting onto them what we really hate in ourselves. Realizing this takes some time dedicated to inner work, often asking a friend to assist in discernment; but the spiritual peace that can result is well worth it.

We will have many guides along the way, and will find ourselves called to practice discernment over and over again. The ultimate hope is to see the Christ, the God within each other. A therapist can help us deal with the shadow side of ourselves. And our spiritual director keeps reminding us to look for the God, the Christ in our neighbor. This is more likely to occur when we learn to stay connected to the Christ within ourselves.

Charleston: Changed Again

"I have been changed. I am not the same person I was before. Over time, over many experiences, good and bad, I have grown in understanding, awareness and compassion. I have found a deeper sense of peace. I have come to appreciate the importance of love."—Bishop Steven Charleston Daily Facebook Page.

I know we are called to articulate our truth as best we can; but then I realize that we must let it go. This is hard, because the life approach we have been taught has been like a *dog with a bone* about issues we are passionate about. I try to turn the situation over, to give up the "bone."

Nevertheless, it is hard to give up our admiration of people who are like that faithful *Border Collie with a bone* about issues they believe in. Many of us have realized the cost to our own body, mind, and soul of holding onto that bone. We may find it difficult to achieve peace, to hold on to love. Our arteries tighten up. When we lose, we think we must try harder. When we win, we strive harder to keep doing it better.

This is my hope for change: That we will no longer see life as win or lose. Rather, we have a part: We are to step out of our comfort zone and speak out in love and try to make a difference. More and more we know that for every cross there is a resurrection. God brings about the resurrection, rolls away the stone. Our job is to keep looking and listening for every possible sign of love and resurrection.

We will have setbacks in giving up this control, thinking we are responsible for the resurrection; but stark situations that remind us we are not in charge will repeatedly bring us back to the truth. Believing that we have control of situations in our lives and in the world of others is *fake news*, a fantasy; but there is this sweet voice that whispers in ours ears, continually telling us *we have such magnificent ideas* and need to be a powerful person who always accomplishes our agenda.

If we recognize ourselves as connected to something greater than us—then we acknowledge there may be a better plan than our own …that a strong person may be one who pauses and perhaps prays and listens before she speaks …does the best she can …and then gives up the results to God, who may have a better view of the situation than she does. Amazing.

Recovery Conference 2018

"Hope is being able to see that there is light despite all of the darkness."—Desmond Tutu.

I am attending the Episcopal Recovery Conference in Asheville, North Carolina, and learning so much about recovery from addictions. First, I realize that the longer I am in recovery, the more I think I know and have heard it all. Today I am disabused of this thought process. I actually know very little. That is why it is important to continue to attend gatherings like this.

One speaker, Chris Budnick, executive director of Healing Transitions in Raleigh, talks about how we think recovery for others should look similar to ours. Not true. Recovery from addiction is not a cookie cutter process. We share with others our experience, strength, and hope; but we must not expect others to have *the same* experience, strength, and hope. Perhaps we can see this more clearly in reference to our spiritual life. We each have a spiritual connection to God, but it is different for each of us. So also is our response to recovery and our individual path to achieving it.

I learn one more lesson today. We often talk about someone not coming to recovery because he or she "has not hit bottom." That means the person hasn't reached a level of pain that allows openness to change. The speaker gave examples of others who changed because people in recovery kept letting them know there was hope for freedom from addiction. Hope for an alternative life.
Mentors in recovery keep conveying that those who are farther along in recovery care about them, have some realization of what they are

going through, and believe there is hope. Those caught in addiction may see glimpses of new life in the person in recovery who seems honestly to care about them.

This is one more way that those in recovery can carry the message to those who are still suffering: by continuing to reach out and give them hope.

Prejudice and the Daily Office

"Do not let the oppressed be shamed and turned away; never forget the lives of your poor."—*The Daily Office* (www.dailyoffice.wordpress.org).

If I cannot attend the office of Morning Prayer at St. Mark's, I try to read it from this website. If you do not know about this Daily Office website, you are in for a new adventure. When you access it, all the readings for morning, evening, and noonday prayer are right there in front of you. The Lay Vicar, Josh Thomas, also offers hymns and pictures that relate to the readings, as well as prayer petitions that have been submitted. It is not just a website—but a *community of participants* praying during a live, twice-daily service of morning and evening prayer. I always feel connected to pray-ers all over the world when I connect to The Daily Office.

As I read these prayers through this community, my mind takes me out of my own problems, and I move more globally. I see the children and families of Latino origin separated and incarcerated at our southern border. I cannot stop thinking and praying about them and those who are making and supporting policies that affect them.

Then I remember an episode yesterday from our food pantry. I go to St. Mark's weekly food pantry just to meet and talk with those who come for their groceries. I see a brown-skinned woman with black hair and three children of similar appearance come in. They seem confused about the process. I immediately think they must be Latino, and motion to our member who speaks Spanish to help them.

The mother tells him she speaks English. Later, as I talk with the children, I find out that they are Native American.

I learn about my own prejudice, thinking all brown-skinned people must be of a certain heritage. I cannot condone the prejudice of those who are harming immigrant children and their families who are seeking asylum in our country; but because of this incident, I gain a brief insight into my own darkness.

I make amends to the family and hope I have learned some life lessons taught to me by those who were here in this land long before me.

Palmer: Violence

"Violence is what happens when we don't know what else to do with our suffering."—Parker Palmer in *On the Brink of Everything: Grace, Gravity & Getting Old* (Berrett-Koehler Publishers, Inc., 2018), p. 48.

I am not even one quarter the way through this recent book by Parker Palmer and already have underlined most of what I have read. I am especially moved by this quote about violence from Parker's commencement address to the class of 2015 at Naropa University in Boulder, Colorado.

We daily see this in our lives. Violence comes from accumulated suffering that we and generations before us can no longer bear. Violence is grief that cannot find any other outlet or transformation. Maybe we have just inherited this way to respond to grief. Violence is grief over the loss of identity, loss of what we think may be ours, loss over loved ones, loss of land, loss of life's work, loss of the rights that others have, loss of food and shelter, loss of love.

Grief is a powerful energy. I know it best in working with people in a grief recovery group, Walking the Mourner's Path. Grief saps us of all energy. We at times become paralyzed. When we are grieving, we can become violent toward others, blaming them for the loss of our loved one. We can become violent to ourselves, growing bitter, seeing ourselves as victims.

There is hope, great hope. I have seen this enormous energy turn into something other than violence. As we listen to the stories of others who are suffering, this impulse can be transformed into empathy and love. When suffering moves away from its own pain and reaches out to the pain of others, it can become compassion. Compassion leads to nonviolent ways to move through the suffering, especially in community.

Suffering may not be the only factor in violence, but it can help to look at violence in ourselves and in the world to see what part suffering plays in these interactions. This involves looking at what must be going on in ourselves and others, showing compassion whenever violence raises its ugly head.

Our faith stories teach us that finding love and compassion out of suffering can lead to a resurrection experience.

Feminine Wisdom

"To the disciples who were always asking for words of wisdom, the Master said, 'Wisdom is not expressed in words. It reveals itself in action.' But when he saw them plunge headlong into activity, he laughed and said, 'That isn't action. That's motion.'"—Anthony de Mello.

There is a Greek myth about Psyche and Eros that many people doing Jungian work use to describe women's growth in consciousness. The story is the basis for *She* by Robert Johnson and *Till We Have Faces* by C. S. Lewis. In order for Psyche to reunite with her lover, Eros, she is given several tasks. At the beginning of each task, Psyche collapses and weeps as she sees that the task is insurmountable.

My image is Psyche lying on one of those old-fashioned fainting couches that every woman of means once possessed—with her hand turned palm up on her forehead, her eyes closed, and her head leaning backwards on or off the couch. It is the feminine body language of surrender and stillness.

Instead of plowing directly into an arduous task before us, the feminine energy in each of us waits, rests. In the waiting, answers come that are completely out of the box. They are truly answers to prayer. Some would say these solutions are received from the Spirit of God within her. Help comes from places she never imagined.

This is wisdom: the action of waiting, stillness, especially before we are asked to do something we do not think we can do.

I remember waiting in an outer office before a difficult meeting with other physicians. At first it upset me that I, this important person, had to wait! Slowly I realized that the waiting was a gift, wisdom from a mysterious source. It was a time to quiet myself, to surrender to the moment, and to be still before going into this difficult meeting. When I could do this, I carried with me the feminine energy of staying in relationship with those around me. This made all the difference.

Humility

"Do not imagine that if you meet a really humble man he will be what most people call 'humble' nowadays: he will not be a sort of greasy, smarmy person, who is always telling you that, of course, he is nobody. Probably all you will think about him is that he seemed a cheerful, intelligent chap who took a real interest in what you said to him."—C. S. Lewis in *Mere Christianity*.

Frederick Buechner in *Beyond Words* (HarperOne, 2009) also talks about humility as not thinking *ill* of ourselves—but simply not assuming that we are more important than others. We are not more significant or less essential than our neighbor in God's eyes. This definition of humility does not devalue ourselves, but values ourselves and others on the same plane. The humble person is genuinely interested in others and their well-being because he or she has a sound sense of self and does not need accolades from others in order to survive.

John McQuiston II in *Always We Begin Again* (Skylight Paths, 2004), his modernization of the Rule of Benedict, describes Benedict's twelve stages of humility. This explanation differs greatly from what we have been taught about being humble. If we are to follow the Rule and to have humility, we must realize the sacredness of each moment. We acknowledge that being guided only by our own self-will can lead us astray. In our humility we will speak gently and briefly, accepting our limitations, being patient, not hiding our faults, being content, and refraining from judgment. We can never be joyful over the problems, disappointments, and losses of others.

Three writers from different ages agree in telling us that humility is important in our life in community and in our own individual development.

All Saints: Generous Heart, Columbus

"God give me a generous spirit in all I say and do, generous in my words to speak kindly of others, generous in my forgiveness to restore relationships, generous in my support to those in need around me. Let my generosity not be an occasional act, but a way of life, the core from which my behavior emerges, generous in praise, patience and prayer."—Bishop Steven Charleston Daily Facebook Page.

Today on All Saints Day I remember "Columbus," someone well known by all in the recovery community in Little Rock, Arkansas, only by his first name. Every year, usually early in the morning on the birthday of your sobriety, you received a phone call from Columbus. You waited in anticipation for that call, celebrating one more year of an alternative life with someone you knew only over the phone lines.

Columbus' wife of forty-six years would leave him three times before he went into his last rehabilitation, after many DUIs and missed work, and days when she admitted not knowing where he was. Columbus died in the thirty-eighth year of his sobriety and was credited with having led to sobriety thousands of men and women all over the world.

Columbus made 15,000 calls a year and almost half a million calls before his death. He also called people he knew were no longer in recovery and told them he cared about them. Many people say they returned to recovery because of Columbus.

Columbus' wife described his change when he went into recovery as "truly unbelievable. He became a dedicated and involved father and grandfather after he came so close to losing his family."

When I hear people wonder what they could possibly do to make a difference in the world, I tell them Columbus' story: one man with a generous heart, picking up the phone every day, and changing lives with a simple phone call. One Day at a Time.

This may be the way saints live. They are resurrection people. They know what Good Friday is like. They change themselves and bring resurrection into the world one day at a time.

Charleston: All Faithful Departed

"You have heard the whispers on quiet summer evenings when you have been walking alone. They are the sound of the ancestors, speaking softly just on the other side of what we call real. You have seen the strange lights at twilight, like candles lit in evening rooms, beckoning people home to houses you cannot see. You have felt the touch on your shoulder, when you were deep in prayer or bent with worry, and known the energy that hums along the wires of faith, the presence of a power that knows how to heal. You have experienced the physical mystery that surrounds us, the mystery of the Spirit, the thousand tiny proofs that we live next door to heaven, waking up in a wonder we are only beginning to discover."—Bishop Steven Charleston Daily Facebook Page (10/31/2018).

November 1st was All Saints' Day, and November 2nd was The Celebration of All Faithful Departed. These two liturgical celebrations are our Church's *family* reunion day. It is the time for us to pull out our family photograph album and remember where we came from and all the faithful who influenced our lives.

Where were you the night of April 4, 1968? My husband and I were seniors in medical school in Memphis. That night Martin Luther King was assassinated outside of the Lorraine Motel. Memphis became a police state. Clergy in Memphis responded by marching to the office of the mayor, Henry Loeb, to ask for relief for the striking sanitation workers whose cause had brought King to Memphis. The ministers gathered at St. Mary's Episcopal Cathedral. At the last moment, Dean William Dimmick, who later became the bishop of Northern Michigan (and eventually baptized our two sons), went into the Cathedral and took down the processional cross from the high altar. Holding it high above him (he was a very short man), he led the march down Poplar Avenue to City Hall.

The air was electric. Down the streets, the clergy and supporters marched. A Methodist minister writes about one moment he will never forget: As the clergy are advancing down Poplar Avenue, up ahead, he sees an elderly woman sitting on her front porch. As the procession approaches her, she stands up and screams, "GET THAT CROSS BACK IN THE CHURCH WHERE IT BELONGS!"[1]

Dean Dimmick took the cross out of the cathedral into the streets of a city on the verge of riot. He taught us where Christ lives, especially in times of grief and oppression. Christ is out in the midst of the mess. Christ was out walking the streets of Memphis in 1968.

Today my prayer is that we will be able to emulate what we learned from Dean Dimmick and take Christ out to those who are sick and suffering, to those who are hungry, to those living in poverty, to victims and families of the many recent episodes of violence in our country, to immigrants around the world, to the lonely and fearful, to those who may be invisible to us much of the time.

On the days we remembering saints, we especially affirm what we cannot explain. Dean Dimmick will always be there beside us, praying and cheering us on.

[1]Katherine Moorehead, "Stepping Out of the Tent" in *Preaching Through the Year of Mark* (Morehouse, 1999), p. 75.

Beauty and Meaning

"By its very nature life is full of meaning, for the God who said 'let there be light' also proclaimed it good. And the God who said 'let us make humankind' also blessed us and proclaimed us to be very good indeed."—Brother James Koester, SSJE, from "Brother, Give Us a Word," a daily email sent to friends and followers of the Society of Saint John the Evangelist (SSJE.org).

We are gathered this weekend for the seventh year with a group of friends who meet once a year on the top of Petit Jean Mountain to give thanks for Camp Mitchell, the camp and conference center for the Episcopal Church in Arkansas. Our bishop celebrates Eucharist with us; we learn about what has been happening at the camp over the past year; and we hear about new volunteer opportunities while raising money for a project for the new year. We have paved roads and paths for those who are handicapped, remodeled buildings, remodeled a kitchen, built an event deck, and contributed to a farm program; but mostly we hope to educate people about the camp so they can go back home to remind others of this natural jewel.

Our camp has changed lives, especially those of our children and youth. This is where so many have met God.

The camp is strategically built on the brow of a small mountain overlooking the Arkansas River Valley and the Arkansas River. In the early morning, clouds fill the valley and we cannot help but feel we are indeed in heaven. Each evening, the sunset paints a new pink and orange and red panoramic skyscape that no other artist has been able to duplicate. Indian caves with their faint markings live below, while three-hundred-million-year-old fossil rocks lie beside us at every turn as reminders that life was here long before we were.

Every inch of nature on the mountain is spectacular; but living in dwellings on the brow is not an easy life for humans. The wind and rain and electrical storms take their toll. The upkeep on these habitats is high. So that is why we come together to give thanks and care for the gift we have been given.

We are actually paying it forward to care for a place that has changed our lives—to preserve it for those who are coming after us, most of whom we will never know. The beauty of Petit Jean Mountain has not only brought us closer to the God of our understanding, but has been one of our best teachers about stewardship. We learn by caring for a precious pearl of great price that we have been privileged to view for a nanosecond of its existence.

I will keep permanently in my mind this image from our opening Eucharist just after the sun set last night. We light candles around the altar of our open-air chapel to remind us to give thanks for all those who were here before us who cared for this land. We also light candles to pray for our children and grandchildren and great-grandchildren who will come to enjoy and preserve this holy ground long after we are gone.

We look forward to being back again, to renew our lives and give thanks for this sacred mountain.

Remembering World War I

"This is a war to end all wars."—Woodrow Wilson.

This week we remembered the 101st anniversary of the end of World War I, the Great War, the War to End All Wars. The war officially ended on the 11th hour of the 11th day of the 11th month. Last year at 11 on November 11th or Veterans Day in the morning, bells tolled in churches all over the globe. Special programs about the war were held around the world, most notably in England and in Paris, France, where the world's diplomats met to commemorate the peace accord that ended the war.

Both of my grandfathers served in the war and came home. I never heard one grandfather speak of his experience. The other, Grandfather Whaley, rarely talked about the war itself, but did have a lot to say about his experience in the army. He was born in what is now the Great Smokey Mountain National Park. Going into the armed service was his higher education.

When I was in college, my grandfather wrote to me every week on his old typewriter, on which several keys would often get stuck. The lines of type were uneven. Every letter, however, was full of his army experiences and how he related it to my new life in college. He would remind me that the best lessons were found in the people I would meet and the places where I would travel. Almost every sentence ended with etc., etc., etc.

I kept every one of his letters. The girls on my floor in my dorm would gather each week to hear about his wisdom from his life experiences a half-century earlier in the army in World War I—and about his present life in small-town Virginia.

Did I forget to tell you also that my grandfather always enclosed a dollar bill with each letter?

Election Day

"For an Election

Almighty God, to whom we must account for all our powers
and privileges: Guide the people of the United States in the election
of a president and other officials and representatives;
that, by faithful administration and wise laws, the rights of
all may be protected and our nation be enabled to fulfill your
purposes; through Jesus Christ our Lord. *Amen."—Book of Common
Prayer, p. 822.*

It is hard not to think about the election today. I remember
all those who are running for office, some I know personally. I have
looked through a small window to see what a noble sacrifice it has
been for some of them. It has been a sacrifice for their family, for
their bodies, for their minds, for their hearts, and for their spirits.

How difficult it must be for candidates to stay with their core
values through the entire experience. How hard it must be to stay
truthful. We see this at every turn. We hear people saying things they
did and will do after the election which we know never happened and
will never happen.

It is a great price to pay, to win, but to lose one's integrity. More than
any other people, politicians may be susceptible to bribes coming in
the form of people with deep pockets who offer money to the
candidate for them to support their programs or businesses. Winning
becomes so expensive or so important that all other values may go to
the wayside. May this be a lesson for all of us in our own lives as we
are tempted to compromise to reach a goal.

Our Daughters of the King will pray in St. Mark's chapel all day while the polls are open for all of those running for office today. They all so need our prayers. We give thanks for their courage to stand up and try to make a difference in this world, often at significant sacrifice.

We pray for all of us that we will be able to accept the results of the election and continue to pray for those who did not win as well as those who will be the winners.

We also must pray that all who are elected to office will be able to keep their core values and become the people they say they are and the people God created them to be.

While we are at it, let us pray the same prayer for ourselves.

Joseph of Arimathea and the Election

"He was a good and righteous man …and had not agreed to their plan and action. He came from the Jewish town of Arimathea and he was waiting expectantly for the kingdom of God."—Luke 23:50-51.

As we read this, all of us will know most of the results of this midterm election. Our prayers should be with those who win the election, for those who lose, and for those who voted for either side.

For some reason, I am hoping to remember Joseph of Arimathea after this election. "He was a good and righteous man …and had not agreed to their plan and action. He came from the Jewish town of Arimathea and he was waiting expectantly for the kingdom of God." *That's us!!* I think we all are waiting *expectantly* for the kingdom of God and are hoping to find some part of it in all the people we voted for. We have much in common with Joseph of Arimathea.

"He *did not* agree to their plan and action." But *what* DID he do about it? Did he speak up for Jesus? There is no record that anyone testified on Jesus' behalf at his mock trial. We have sometimes been like Joseph of Arimathea—when we see *injustice* and wrongdoings in the lives of others and ourselves, but we do not speak up against them. We fear what might happen to us. We dread the consequences of speaking out. We fear what we do or say might be offensive and hurt someone, or—heaven forbid—we would become unpopular. We are afraid that our voice will not make a difference.

But then a transformation occurs in Joseph, what we might call *a moment of clarity*. Joseph personally goes to Pilate. What bravery. He asks for Jesus' body, personally and compassionately takes the nails out of Jesus' hands and feet, washes the blood from his head, hands, feet, side, and back, wraps the body in a linen cloth, and lays Jesus in what presumably was his own tomb.

Are we Joseph of Arimathea? Is there a point at which we can no longer live our lives concerned only about our own well-being, focused on issues that affect only us? We no longer pretend to go along with the old crowd inside and outside of ourselves. We look to our inner core values and speak our truth and act on it. This certainly happens for people in recovery from addictions and for spiritual friends seeking a deeper connection to God.

This also may be how we experienced voting recently. No matter the results of the election, we voted and let our voice be heard. We took a stand. For many of us, as with Joseph, it was only a beginning.

Think about it. We who are gathered today through the internet know what it is like to be Joseph of Arimathea. I believe there is a Joseph of Arimathea inside each of us, finally making a stand, changing the way we have been relating to ourselves, to God, and to the world—speaking out with love and compassion, becoming concerned for the plight of others.

Remember the quiet, compassionate, loving courage of Joseph of Arimathea that is in each of us, the courage to change, the determination to foster love and understanding between ourselves and others. We need that kind of courage to bring compassionate healing to our country, especially in the days ahead.

Joseph provided the tomb for resurrection to take place. That is now our job. We have learned about resurrection and compassion through spiritual friends and in the thin places where we worship. We are called now to be that same vessel for compassion and resurrection out in the world today, where reconciliation is so desperately needed in our divided world—perhaps even more now than before the election.

Let us be that place for healing and resurrection.

Two Spiritual Approaches

"Darkness is not dark for you, and night shines as the day. Darkness and light are but one."—Psalm 139:12.

Richard Rohr in his daily emails[1] describes the two traditional approaches to God as "dark" and "light." The more cognitive, formal, theological approach is called the *kataphatic* way. In it we reach God by learning and studying the divine, practicing an ascent to the sacred, reaching for the light. This has been the most followed approach to God since the Protestant Reformation and the Age of Enlightenment. We could describe it as the way of knowledge or knowing God.

The other spiritual tradition or way of seeking God is the *apophatic* way, in which we move beyond words and rational knowing into silence. This is the contemplative approach to the mystery, the "not-knowing." It is a descent into the dark, into the unknown sacred within.

Rohr emphasizes how important both ways of seeking God are for a balanced spiritual life. Those whose personality type involves more thinking and sensing, making decisions based on concrete, rational, reasonable facts, will be drawn to the *kataphatic,* or ascent approach. Those whose personality leans more toward feeling and intuitive functions, who make decisions based on relationships, considering many connections and patterns, may be more drawn to the descending *apophatic* or inward approach.

Many involved in spiritual direction suggest that we try to use the approach opposite to our tendencies during Advent and Lent. For example, if we are a thinking person, we are to try contemplative prayer. If we are a feeling and intuitive person, we should consider putting our toe into the water by studying our tradition, sacred Scripture, or the writings of significant theologians.

Just a suggestion to *think* or *wonder* about.

[1]Richard Rohr, Center for Action and Contemplation. Daily Meditation, "Darkness and Light," adapted from Richard Rohr's *Things Hidden: Scripture as Spirituality* (Franciscan Media, 2008), pp. 115-116.

Vulnerable

"The only choice we have as we mature is how to inhabit our vulnerability ..."—David Whyte.

Vulnerability. Poet David Whyte gives us one word to take with us today. Vulnerability, however, does not live alone, but resides in a word community.

Intimacy. Another word that lives with vulnerability. We allow someone whom we trust to see and hear our inner thoughts and concerns, our highs and lows.

Humility is also a close family member of this word community. We don't think of ourselves as any better than someone else.

Humanness whispers in the ear of vulnerability. We are to take off our mask of "perfection." We are to admit our mistakes to others promptly and to learn from them.

Forgiveness must also be a beloved companion of vulnerability. We are to ask for forgiveness when we have wronged others and be ready to forgive ourselves for our own mistakes.

Vulnerability, intimacy, humility, humanness, forgiveness are five construction workers in a family business crucial for the building of our own Habitat for Humanity.

Wounds

"The reality is that every human being is broken and vulnerable. How strange that we should ordinarily feel compelled to hide our wounds when we are all wounded!"—M. Scott Peck in *The Different Drum* (Touchstone, 1998).

Our experience tells us that when we share our woundedness, we become less vulnerable. We no longer must pretend we are something that we are not or in essence wear a mask, which takes up an enormous amount of energy. We now can employ all that energy just to be ourselves, to become the person God created us to be. We become more human. In turn, others share their wounds because they recognize us as a safe place—another human being who may have just an inkling of what pain is all about.

Letting others know we are human and have pain and make mistakes is also a path into the divine within ourselves and others. This is the path we all are seeking. There is a wide, gaping entrance to this path that opens through our wounds, into the Christ, the Holy, the Spirit within each other.

This is the path from Good Friday to Resurrection.

Where Is God?

"God is in the kitchen, sitting quietly over a cup of coffee. God is on the street corner, waiting for the light to change. God is at the bar, watching the game on TV. God is in the beauty shop, listening to the latest stories. There is no place where we are that God is not."—Bishop Steven Charleston Daily Facebook Page.

I sometimes share with spiritual friends this short writing by Bishop Steven Charleston from his daily Facebook Page, when they cannot seem to find any answers to the question, "So, where do you see God working in your life?" I suggest an exercise at the end of the day of writing down places they have been, people they have met and would like to remember, and any feelings or thoughts about the presence of God during their day. It is important to write it down if possible. Writing takes things out of our body and mind and into our tangible world. Some think it is silly and never do it. Others find it helpful to begin to see and feel a connection they think they have lost that is always there, right beside them, all day…and night.

The church at which I serve is on a corner with a stoplight. Recently our family minister, Luke, started putting a short "stoplight prayer" on our church's electronic sign by the stoplight. We weekly hear of people whose day changes when they stop just for a second to connect to our God, who is always there. Briefly stopping what we are doing and noticing creation around us is our first step out of ourselves and into the life of knowing and feeling the perpetual presence of God.

Charleston: Heart String

"Here is something to do for the little kids in your life. When you are saying goodbye, make a special moment of showing them that you are tying something to their wrist. Tell them it is a heart string. You can't see it, but if you close your eyes you will know it is there. It will stay on their wrist wherever they go so your love will always be with them. And not to worry, it is magic string, so it will never get tangled, never knock anything over, and never break. It will just keep you connected in your hearts so your love for one another will always be there."—Bishop Steven Charleston Daily Facebook Page (9/13/18).

Several of our recent Sunday Scripture readings have been about little children and entering the kingdom of God. Jesus tells us in Mark (10:2-26), Luke (18:15-17), and Matthew (19:14), that we must enter the kingdom by receiving it like little children.

Bishop Charleston's heart string message to children not only reminds us how we stay connected to those we love, but *how God stays connected to us.* The God string is always there, even if we cannot feel it. At times it feels like a thick rope, and at other times like the thinnest of sewing threads. Sometimes we feel so close to God that we could reach out and touch the Holy One; and sometimes our God seems nowhere to be found.

Almost always we can feel our God connection when we go outside and realize there is something, some power much greater than we can imagine. We still may not believe that this power affirms us or cares about us until a call, a visit, a note from someone else brings God's love to us. Sometimes that person tells us he or she is praying for us, and we feel those prayers. Then we in time again feel God's love and can only respond by returning that love to another as it was given to us.

What Matters Most

"The things that matter most in our lives are not fantastic or grand. They are moments when we touch one another, when we are there in the most attentive or caring way."—Jack Kornfield in *A Path with Heart* (Bantam, 1993).

This morning I am remembering when we returned from my almost sixty-year high school reunion. There were thirty-three in my graduating class. We thought we could make the trip that year, but weren't sure about the next, so decided to go now. We had lunch with friends I knew growing up in a small town in tidewater Virginia. Some might have called it a one-horse town, since we only had one stop light. We would talk about driving up to "the light." I am so glad we went. I talked with one of my friends who now lives in a county in Virginia that boasts it has no stop lights!

It was as if it had been only a few days since we last saw each other—instead of fifty-eight years. Why is it so easy to re-connect to those we grew up with? They knew us before we had many masks. There is no need to have pretensions around them. They know who we are and where we came from. Meeting again, we are all back on an equal playing field.

The majority of the women in my class went off to college. Many of the boys stayed in our small town, worked at the mill, and took early retirement. All seemed to enjoy life. Most seemed genuinely interested in what the others were doing and asked about them rather than talking about themselves. All had had some tragedy, and all had had some magical moments.

Shortly after we returned that year, my oldest granddaughter sent us pictures of her senior prom. I see pictures of her friends, and can in some small way understand how important these relationships must be to her. I wonder what her fifty-eighth high school reunion will be like.

I will keep that day and this visit in the memory book of my mind and hope to revisit it again, hopefully next year, giving thanks for where I grew up and the many friends who influenced me and taught me about caring.

Learning in Community, Expectations

"The need for connection and community is primal, as fundamental as the need for air, water, and food."—Dean Ornish.

There is no question that we learn about ourselves, others, and God in community. We find the Christ within ourselves when we see it in others and that love reflects back to us. We learn how to get out of our own world, which can become stifling, by reaching out to those around us. We become aware of our defects and sins by first seeing them in others and being repulsed by them. Finally, we realize these sins are also in ourselves.

We also learn about our gifts as we admire those gifts in others and one day realize they also may be in us.

In a recent writing by Bill Shiflett from Church of the Saviour[1], we learned some more about ourselves in relationship to our expectations of others. Shiflett believes that what we are seeking in others may at times be *our own* personal expectations projected onto another, thereby making that person responsible for something that is really in, or needed in, ourselves. My experience is that this can be an easy trap for parents and even grandparents. What we are hoping our child will do is really something that *we* want to do.

This rang true to me many years ago when I was talking to a spiritual friend, Peggy Hays, and telling her about something I was hoping one of my children would do. Whenever we talked about it, she would always say, "What is it that *you* want to do?" It took me years to finally "get it."

What does this mean in spiritual direction? Many people come for spiritual direction because they are having difficulty with the clergy of their church or with another spiritual friend, and this relationship is interfering with their own spirituality. They have expectations of the clergy and of their friends that are not being fulfilled. Certainly, there are times when these expectations are realistic and represent ministry that the clergy specifically are called to do. My experience, however, is that it is always important to examine whether we are projecting onto someone an expectation or a calling or a need that actually applies to ourselves.

I remember a longtime priest my husband and I dearly loved. We moved away and lost connection with the church because we could not find a relationship with similar clergy in our new town. We had expectations that our new priest would be similar to the one with whom we were so close.

We do need a community to connect to God; but the paradox is that our connection to God should not depend on our relationship with someone else.

[1]Bill Shiflett, "Assumptions," Daily Quote, InwardOutward.org, Church of the Saviour, Washington, D. C. (7/18/2018).

Thanksgiving, Listening Day

"To listen is very hard, because it asks of us so much interior stability that we no longer need to prove ourselves by speeches, arguments, statements, or declarations. True listeners no longer have an inner need to make their presence known. They are free to receive, to welcome, to accept. Listening is a form of spiritual hospitality by which you invite strangers to become friends, to get to know their inner selves more fully, and even to dare to be silent with you."—Henri Nouwen in *Bread for the Journey* (HarperSanFrancisco, 1997).

As we gather today with family and friends, this is the perfect time to sit back and listen. Listening is at the heart of being a spiritual friend. Nouwen reminds us that listening does not mean waiting for our turn to talk. Instead, it is letting someone else know you are offering the gift of your energy and time to be present and attentive.

Some think it may be easier for introverts, but in reality, introverts may still process what they want to say in their minds while others are talking, and therefore they are only pseudo-listening. Extroverts may have difficulty responding directly to what they are hearing, for they process what they hear on the outside.

The answer is practicing engaged repetition. This is an art form that must be practiced consciously every day until it becomes as unconscious as brushing our teeth.

We have grown up in a multitasking world where we learn to do many things simultaneously: eating while we work or watch television, working on several projects, seeking to solve multiple problems at a time, looking at emails, texting and searching on our iPhones while we are sitting down to meet with others. While someone is talking to us, we may be thinking of how we will solve another problem as soon as we move on to the next person or meeting.

Living in the present and active listening are becoming lost arts. We must practice them intentionally. My experience is that making eye contact helps keep us focused on the person or people to whom we are listening. This enables us actively to "look for" the Christ *visibly* and *invisibly* within others—who can truly be revealed only as we begin to see the Christ within ourselves. This is a major disadvantage of "listening" to what someone says on social media. We cannot make eye contact or observe what people are saying with their body language.

Listening is an art form and a gift. St. Benedict calls it "listening with the ear of our heart." Margaret Guenther calls it *Holy Listening.*

Happy Thanksgiving and Happy Listening Day from our family to yours.

Mortality

"On the death of a friend, we should consider that the fates through confidence have devolved on us the task of a double living, that we have henceforth to fulfill the promise of our friend's life also, in our own, to the world."—Henry David Thoreau.

We are at our fiftieth medical school reunion. One of the most surprising developments that I never envisioned is the number of those in our class who have died. We were invincible, ready to take on whatever came at us. We had overcome almost every possible hardship, abuse, prejudice, poverty, humiliation, ridicule, and whatever else was presented to us. We knew how to work without sleep, be shamed by what we did not know in front of peers, and read and study until it seemed our eyes were coming out.

But death was never part of our own plan. It was something that happened to those we were not able to save with our medical skills and knowledge.

We walked constantly with death and still remember every face of those we could not keep alive because of our own ignorance, or because the medical science that could save them had not yet been developed. We never imagined that those with whom we worked so closely, sharing a common experience, would now not be alive. How did they die? Was it a lengthy illness? We search for their obituaries: Ken, Jim, Charles.

Of course, this has been a wake-up call about our own mortality. There is always the question of why are we still alive and they are not. Did we take better care of ourselves or do we have better genes? Today I know that most of the answers are out of our reach.

More and more we have to live into mystery. What we do feel is a desire to give thanks for those with whom we weathered a wilderness adventure. Somehow each of them contributed to how we have developed into the person God created us to be. We send prayers of thanksgiving to them for how their lives touched ours. We also ask for their prayers until we at some time will again be connected to them and learn even more about each other. We look forward to continuing our journey together along with the God of our understanding, surrendering, trying to live one day at a time, being grateful for each day, enjoying the journey without having to know all the answers.

Nouwen: Leadership

"It is the compassionate authority that empowers, encourages, calls forth hidden gifts, and enables great things to happen. True spiritual authorities are located in the point of an upside-down triangle, supporting and holding into the light everyone they offer their leadership to."—Henri Nouwen in *Bread for the Journey* (HarperSanFrancisco, 1997).

The upside-down triangle. What a brilliant image for leadership, a leadership that supports, empowers, and encourages those being led. I have a spiritual friend who tells me that his senior warden explained it another way: "You have to let them know that you care before you show them what you know." How true this is in any kind of relationship or ministry. This is one of the models Jesus gives us. I think I have encountered a handful of leaders in my lifetime who fit this description. It is a rare form of leadership. It is servant leadership.

Just recently I cried with another friend, Ann, as we shared the struggles of trying to lead through practicing this leadership style. When we use it, often we are called a "weak sister." This type of leadership is counter culture. We can find ourselves met with resistance at almost every turn.

Even if we ourselves have not been a servant leader in the past, there is still time to change. When we are given the chance, we can try to live it. We can share our experience with other spiritual friends and support each other. It is a leadership model that is not powered by our ego—or by as little ego as possible.

Parker Palmer identifies this form of leadership in *Let Your Life Speak* (Jossey-Bass, 1999). These leaders are not insecure about their own identity, depriving others of their autonomy to buttress or support their own. The identity of these leaders does not depend on the role they play or the power over others it gives them.

May we pray to become this kind of servant leader, and that we will be led to role models and mentors who also embody it.

Nouwen: The Challenge of Aging

"Waiting patiently in expectation does not necessarily get easier as we become older...As we grow in age we are tempted to settle down in a routine way of living and say: 'Well, I have seen it all. ...There is nothing new under the sun. ...I am just going to take it easy and take the days as they come.' But in this way our lives lose their creative tension. We no longer expect something really new to happen. We become cynical or self-satisfied or simply bored."—Henri Nouwen

I am thinking of the normal routine of so many people our age. Many think they deserve to rest because they have worked so hard for so many years. But I am learning there are many forms of rest. We can sit and talk or watch movies with our grandchildren. Eventually we will tell our story to them. This, I think, is one of our greatest ministries to let those who will live on after us know the story of our family. My experience is they may not be interested in hearing unless we are doing something together, becoming their friend, not just being their grandparent. My husband tells family stories occasionally as he takes our grandchildren to school. He doesn't do it every day or they might become bored! We can be story tellers while fishing or walking, hiking or crafting or fixing dinner or eating meals together. Telling our family story gives our children and grandchildren roots, roots which connect them to a loving God. It also helps us to recount our own story and the purpose of our own life and our roots.

Do not be discouraged if family members are not interested. Consider writing or making an oral video of your story. Often after we have died, maybe not until members of our family are our age do they become interested. My experience is that the older we become, the more we look for our roots. It is a way of grounding ourselves, connecting us to the earth from which we came and will return. This also becomes a story where we, ourselves, still find even more awareness. As we tell our story, we begin to realize how a loving God worked in our life and the lives of our family at every turn, every day. We may only comprehend this when in time we share the history of our family and how God and God's love was and is with us at every turn.

Parker Palmer: *On the Brink*

"I've lost the capacity for multitasking, but I've rediscovered the joy of doing one thing at a time. My thinking has slowed a bit, but experience has made it deeper and richer. I'm done with big and complex projects, but more aware of the loveliness of simple things. . . I like being old because the view from the brink is striking, a full panorama of my life."—Parker Palmer, *On the Brink of Everything: Grace, Gravity & Getting Older*, (Berrett-Koehler Publishers, Inc. 2018) pp. 1-2.

Parker Palmer takes us to the brink of an alternative life. It is a slower life where we have the opportunity to observe and become aware of so much we missed in this world while we were living at a frantic pace: cardinals, dolphins, pelicans, humming birds, downy woodpeckers, Carolina Chickadees, the ocean, crocus, daffodils, old friends. The list goes on. Parker Palmer has many suggestions for our new life. We are to consider being a mentor, knowing we will learn as much or more from the one we mentor. We are to be more observant of our world outside of us and inside our inner world.

Palmer reminds us that "violence happens when we do not know what else to do with our suffering." We are therefore still called to reach out with love to those who suffer and become acquainted with our own suffering and what we can learn from it. Parker Palmer asks us still to welcome everything, the good and bad that comes into our lives. He quotes Rumi's poem, "The Quest House," reminding us that every part of our life has something to teach us. Palmer talks about how suffering breaks our hearts, but if our heart is supple instead of brittle, it breaks open and allows more love and a fresh life to come in. Our heart becomes supple by stretching it, by taking in all of life's little joys, and by taking in life's little deaths without an anesthetic.

Palmer believes that faith allows us to live with all the contradictions of life. We become faithless when we are so afraid of the contradictions we pretend are not there.

We now have become the observers of our world because most of the rest of the world does not have time to look and digest. They just react. He reminds us that as long as we only look for results, our tasks become smaller and smaller. We are to be seed scatterers. Others may plant, others water. Others reap.

Palmer's experience is that solitude is not being apart from others but being apart from our own self. Palmer reminds us of Benedict's message of "keeping death daily before our eyes." In the meantime, we are to reach out and learn from the younger generation, move toward, not away from what we fear, and spend as much time as possible in the natural world.

Finally, he reminds us how essential humor is as we age, quoting William James: "common sense and a sense of humor are the same thing moving at different speeds."

What We Say

"A year and a half ago my son Griffin, upon turning eighteen, asked me one afternoon, 'Dad, if you could go back in time and say one thing to your eighteen-year-old self, what would it be?' Immediately, my mind began swimming with the possibilities:

'Begin investing in an IRA as soon as you get your first job.'

'Experiences are invariably more enduring and valuable than things.'

'Don't speed. The scenery is worth slowing down to see. Speeding worsens your blood pressure, and speeding tickets destroy your auto insurance premiums.'

All of these nuggets are helpful and borne of experience, but after some additional consideration I realized the one thing I wish my more worldly self could tell my budding, brash, invincible, doe-eyed, thought-I-understood-everything, fragile-and-unknowingly-on-the-precipice, eighteen-year-old self, I would tell myself, 'Barkley, the things we say we cannot unsay.'"—The Very Rev Barkley Thompson, "The Things We Say," Sermon, February 16, 2020, Christ Church Cathedral, Houston, Texas.

Barkley particularly reminds us that our God of love challenges us to bless our family, our friends, our neighbors, and even our enemies. He reminds us that the harm we do with our voice is hard to be unsaid, especially when we use words that are not a blessing but a curse. Barkley reminds us the key is indeed in our breath. When we are considering something that is not a blessing, he suggests we stop and breath in, breath in God's love and also expire or exhale the love of God into the atmosphere. It may take some time before we no longer want to spread out into the universe the unkindness we are considering. Barkley reminds us that this is a spiritual practice, a breath prayer. Done over time, we think and feel differently. Each word of kindness is a part of creation of the God of love we can exhale into our world. My experience is that the stopping is the most important part. I must stop and change gears in my mind and heart and spirit. It may take many breath prayers before I am getting close to breathing out the love of God. I am not going to change the situation or the person who is inducing my anger, but the breath prayer will change me.

I am wondering, like Barkley, what knowledge I would offer to my 18-year-old grandson who just voted for the first time today about what I wish I had done or not done.

Jones: Spiritual Practices

"We all might long for the spiritual direction that Adam received when he walked with God in the Garden …but we live east of Eden."—Tony Jones in *The Sacred Way* (Zondervan, 2005).

Tony Jones has compiled an easily readable compendium of spiritual practices that help us connect to God. The secret of the book is in the subtitle, *Spiritual Practices for Everyday Life*. We do not need to live in a monastery to practice these disciplines. Jones also brings in interesting notes about the history of how each practice began and developed.

The first half of his book covers contemplative practices such as silence, reading, the Jesus Prayer, Centering Prayer, meditation, Ignatian exercises, icons, spiritual direction, and the Daily Office. The second half of the book treats active bodily spiritual practices such as the labyrinth, stations of the cross, pilgrimages, fasting, bodily prayers, Sabbath, and service. Lastly, he writes about developing a Rule of Life, and gives us a short readable bibliography for each practice along with a list of Christian spiritual classics.

Jones' book is restorative, especially when I am feeling disconnected from God. I first reread what he says about the spiritual practices I am using in my rule of life to discover whether I am missing something. Next, I read in Tony's book about a spiritual discipline that I am presently not using but decide to try during this dry period. I also look over his list of books about the disciplines and the classics and pick one out to read. I have recommended the book as a guide for those seeking to become immersed in the spiritual disciplines.

The Sacred Way can be an aid to tasting each practice, perhaps a week or a month at a time. My favorite chapters keep changing. Today I identify most with the section on the Jesus Prayer: "Lord Jesus Christ, Son of God, have mercy on me a sinner." The prayer has been my constant mantra when I am fearful or impatient or meeting with someone with whom I am having difficulty. I identify with Tony Jones when he writes, "The Jesus Prayer has become very significant to me, maybe more than any other practice I've investigated, and it's an important part of my Rule of Life."

All of the Scripture quoted in this book come from New Revised Standard Version (NRSV) of the Bible 1989 unless otherwise noted. Division of Christian Education of the National Council of Churches.

Acknowledgements

This book could not have been completed without the expert help of Isabel Anders and Beth Lambert.

About the Cover: A Myrrh Bearer

"But on the first day of the week, at early dawn, they came to the tomb, taking the spices that they had prepared."
—Luke 24:1

The icon on the cover of this book is from www.uncutmountainsupply.com, maker of Orthodox Christian iconography. This is an image of one of the myrrh bearers, one of the women taking spices to the empty tomb before dawn on an Easter morning. This is what I think Christ calls us to do. We are to bring what is costly to us, our intellect, our feelings, our intuitions, simply our presence, and look for the Christ in the world. We are called to look especially for Christ in those we think are physically and spiritually and mentally dead. We can only find Christ when we give of ourselves, freely, even when we sometimes know it may be dangerous.

We carry with us precious perfumes, costly spices. This is what each of our lives is made up of.

When we have been harmed or have sinned against our neighbor and cannot forgive or accept forgiveness, our life is closed up. We build walls, thick walls, tall walls. We do not want anyone to get in to see our own ugliness or we live in fear that we will be harmed again. We are like a jar filled with this precious oil closed tight. When we accept forgiveness and forgive, we lift up the top and the bottle is opened.

Now myrrh is not the sweet pungent aroma like frankincense. It is earthy, woody, smoky. It is derived from a hardened tree sap.

Myrrh has been used for thousands of years and is mentioned in the Bible over one hundred fifty times. It was used as a natural remedy, an antiseptic to treat wounds, and to purify the dead.

After this oil has been blessed, we might put some in a small dish and use it in a healing service symbolically letting its aroma seep through the walls around our bodies, letting the purify the dead parts of ourselves, letting it heal our wounds and bring us back to a life in the resurrection.

But there is more. Next we are being asked now to go out into the world carrying within us or on us the precious myrrh that was shared with us. We are now myrrh bearers to heal each we see and meet in the world. We are called to bear and carry our healing presence, like the healing power of myrrh, not just at Easter, but in Advent, Christmas, Epiphany, Lent, Pentecost, and in Ordinary Times.

Joanna
Joannaseibert.com
September 2020